# THE RELIGION GAME
## American Style

# THE RELIGION GAME

## American Style

by
Edward Stevens

PAULIST PRESS
New York / Paramus, N.J. / Toronto

Library of Congress
Catalog Card Number: 76-9367

ISBN: 0-8091-1951-X

Published by Paulist Press
*Editorial Office:* 1865 Broadway, N.Y., N.Y. 10023
*Business Office:* 400 Sette Drive, Paramus, N.J. 07652

Printed and bound in the
United States of America

# CONTENTS

Introduction 1

*PART ONE:* THE RELIGION GAME

ONE: Religion in the Reality-Construction Business 13
TWO: Religious Myth as Giver of Meaning 23
THREE: Religious Myth as Giver of Truth 38

*PART TWO:* THE AMERICAN STYLE

FOUR: Faith: The Religious World is Yours to Build 55
FIVE: Human Experience as Religious 70
SIX: A Pragmatic Meaning of God 84
SEVEN: Religious Dynamic for a Functional World Community 100
EIGHT: Religious Liberation: Cracking the Secularist
        Cosmic Egg 115
NINE: Religious Detachment: Surviving in a
        Scarcity Environment 130
Epilogue 143
Notes 149

# INTRODUCTION

As I start to write a book on the philosophy of religion, I feel like a jogger jogging up a hill in the morning just before dawn in the direction of the lone morning star gleaming in the dark and cloudless sky. As I ascend the hill, the bare trees come between me and the star. The star seems to sink behind the trees. The more I increase my pace, the more the star recedes. My star. Myself in lonely pursuit. It is still receding. Soon it will disappear, and I will be jogging on alone in the darkness.

I have no star. There is no star. They have taken away my Lord and I know not where they have laid him. *My* Lord? Yes, mine. In Sri Lanka, children talk easily about Our Lord. They mean, of course, the Lord Buddha. Many people, many lords, many stars: where do they all come from? And the darkness—whence comes the darkness?

The world is a vale of tears. Yes. Each person walks around in cheerful mask and earnest costume carrying secret sadness. But this vale is mercifully a veil, between ourselves and the darkness. Whence comes the darkness? It does not come. It is there. It can even be seen, if your eyesight gets too good. Be careful you do not learn to see well enough to penetrate this shimmering veil through to the abyss it shrouds.

In moments (even hours and days) of emptiness I project, create, an abyss, a darkness. And I fall down and adore the darkness. "I believe in one Lord, the Darkness, who dwells in the Abyss."

As my faith can create a Lord of Darkness and a worship of despair, so too my faith can create a Lord of Light around whom centers my life's hope. Jesus is Lord, proclaims St. Paul. Paul's faith has made this so. "Buddha is Lord," proclaim the Japanese devotees of Amida Buddha, The Compassionate One. Their faith has made this so. Such are the religious worlds of our own making. But they are not the only worlds we make. Sociology of knowledge studies how faith makes and unmakes worlds, and not only religious worlds. Faith makes and unmakes economic worlds. Faith or lack of it, for example, in the British pound sterling can send England's economy reeling or booming. In the course of history, scientific faiths have made the earth the center of the universe, or the sun; they have made the stars into holes in the sky, angelic bodies, or galactic components; the moon has been made into a god, a satellite, and may in the future become a mining outpost for the planet earth.

From generation to generation, we change the rules about how we look at the sun, the economy, morality, politics, or religion. The better you know the rules of the game, the better you can play. A game is not a joke. There is a book out called *The Money Game,* but money—making ends meet—is no joke. Those who understand the rules of the political game rise to the top of the heap. You can call it "playing," but they are playing for keeps. In our own day, even tough realistic science plays its games by different rules. How differently from the orthodox western physician does the Chinese acupuncturist view the human body. At the heart of these two sciences lie different acts of faith, with differing games, and respectively different rules. Again the stakes are high. To whom will you give your faith? Which game will you play? Your health and life hang in the balance.

So this is a book called *The Religion Game: American Style.* Like economics, science, and politics—and perhaps even more than these—religion remains a hard and important fact of human living. To talk about the religion game, as to talk about the money game, is to use a metaphor. The "game" metaphor is not intended to offend but to enlighten. It can help me take an entirely fresh view of the religious side of my life. As with science, politics, and money, the stakes are high: in some religious games, eternal life itself is at issue. Can you stand back and take a fresh hard look at your religion and religious behavior? Can you try to see the different ways in which humans play the religion game? Those play best who understand the rules. It is they who win the prize.

So this book is an invitation to reflect on the religious side of life, with eyes wide open, and taking blindly for granted as little as possible about religion. As in an art gallery, stand back a little. Put some distance between yourself and the picture painted by religious human beings. You are one of the painters who is putting this scene together. What are the others doing? How does your style fit in with theirs? By what rules do you paint, or shall we say play, the religion game? How do the other games relate to yours? Are there rules and games you've never seriously considered? Can you broaden your style of play? Or maybe you will want to play more narrowly and precisely. Do not prejudge the question.

What attitude, then, is appropriate to this inquiry into religion? First, let us avoid putting ourselves into the ecumenism-versus-dogmatism box. There is no particular virtue in being a "bleeding heart ecumenist" rather than a "religious chauvinist pig." Or the other way around, either. Both are concerned with denominational, sectarian, and religious line-drawing. The ecumenist busily erases and fuzzes the borders on the religious map even as the sectarian keeps trying to restore them to their original sharp precision. Both are concerned with *religions* as such, rather than with the *human* as such. This book is an inquiry into the *human* ways of being religious. No religion has a corner on either chauvinists or bleeding hearts. The ecumenism-versus-dogmatism game is only one of the religious games that humans play. It is merely one of the human ways of being religious. Most major religions and minor sects have members who play this particular game with lusty enjoyment. This same game will bore many fellow members who will be at best merely mildly interested spectators, and who will have *their* own religious games, which they play with more zest and interest. In other words, there are many *human* ways of being religious. And this is what our inquiry is all about: religion as a *human* phenomenon.

So this inquiry does not call upon you to deny or suspend your religious commitment or your favorite religious games. A good poker player is more likely to appreciate the game of bridge than would a person who doesn't know how many cards there are in a deck. Religiously, each one of us is standing somewhere, on firm ground or shaky. There is a religious side to most every human life. (You can gather that we are going to have to broaden the definition of "religious" in order to support that statement.) No need, then, to pretend that you are in a religious "no man's land" (unless indeed that is where you are). Let us each try rather to take a reading of where we are. In order to get *there,* one must always start from *here.* Where is the *here* of your religious world? On the other hand, as we examine the various human ways of being religious, the goal is not to somehow incorporate all of these ways into one's own life, to become a religious "Everyman." We need not assume that a world religion, a global ecumenism, would be a religious utopia.

As Kierkegaard has hinted, we must tread the fine line between too much possibility and too much necessity, between excessive ecumenism and excessive dogmatism. Too much possibility (in religious terms: ecumenism run riot) leads to the madhouse. Too much necessity (inflexible dogmatism), on the other hand, is living death.

This book, then, is not a doctor's prescription. There is no intention of evaluating religious games or of improving them. It is rather an observation, an inquiry into a universal human phenomenon. In order to better see and understand it, we must put a certain distance between ourselves and our favorite ways of being religious. But we are not completely disinterested spectators. We are players, too. This commitment of ours can block us from entering with real empathy and understanding into religious games that are very different from our own. But this need not be so, to the extent that we are aware of our preconceptions, prejudgments, prior commitments (in a word, our "*pre*judices"). Aware of them we can be on our guard and take them into account. Understanding their influence on ourselves, we can be in a better position to appreciate the impact of opposite prejudices, opposite religious games, upon the lives of others.

To sum up so far, we have made a statement about the object of inquiry and about our attitude as inquirers. The object of our concern is not *religious,* but *human* ways of being *religious.* Our attitude is not one of uncommitment, but of commitment consciously recognized and taken into account. The game metaphor is meant to embrace both the *distance* we place between ourselves and religion, and at the same time the *commitments* we have at stake as players of the game. Now all we need is a working definition of "religion" (or, better, "religious") in order to get the inquiry off the ground.

Such a working definition must not be too narrow. By accident of birth and education each of us is more intimately acquainted with a particular version of religion. We do not want to reduce the meaning of "religious" to our own peculiar game. Also, so far as possible, we would like a definition of religion that is value-free, biased neither for nor against religion. In this way we can examine religion as a human trait, without prejudging the desirability of this trait. Much evil and much good have been done in the name of religion. We will look at the phenomenon first before making judgments about it. Also, our definition should be open to newly emerging forms of religion. There is no reason to think that this dimension, like the other dimensions of human living, is not in the process of evolution. Finally, we need a definition of religion which is not too broad. Otherwise, it would be meaningless. Let us see why.

In our effort not to be too dogmatic and parochial in our approach to religion, we can fall into the opposite trap. We could be ecumenical to the point of absurdity. There are some Christians, for example, who claim that every human being on earth "deep down" is Christian, whether the individual knows it or not. This is known as the doctrine of "Anonymous Christianity." "Christian" comes to mean the same as "human." It is impossible *not* to be a Christian. Clearly, such a definition of "Christian" is so broad as to lose all meaning. If being human is the only qualification for being Christian, why not just say "human" and be done with it?

Similarly, in our effort to define "religion" we have to be careful not to claim that "deep down" every human being is religious whether recognizing it or not. We would thus fall into what we might call a doctrine of "Anonymous Religiosity." "Religious" would become a synonym for "human." An irreligious or unreligious human would be unthinkable. "Religious" would be evacuated of all meaning. We might just as well say "human" and be done with it. In a word, we need a definition of religion precise enough that it could define some humans as *not* religious.

So my particular religious games form only a part of the worldwide religion game. But the human religious game, in general, can be distinguished from the other games that humans play. The religion game is distinctive in its goal, distinctive in its motivation, and distinctive in the means used to reach its goal. If we can define the goal, the moves, and the motivation for playing, then we can tell who are players and who are not, and can begin our inquiry into the various ways the game is played. So get ready for a definition which is vague enough to include all the human ways of being religious, but precise enough to exclude the games which are not religious.

First, the goal. Unlike other human games, the religious side of man is directly concerned with *what is ultimately real*. Ultimately real—that is vague, all right. Some people call it "God," but let us not narrow it down too quickly. The "ultimate" is that without which nothing else in my life would make sense. It gives meaning to my whole life and every part of it. It is the one thing that makes it worthwhile to go on living, even if all else should fail. It is the one thing that enables me to face my own death, and say "my life has not been in vain." Whatever name I give it, it is the god I worship above all other gods. I may give this supreme and ultimate god a religious sounding name like the Holy, the Tao, Nirvana, the Transcendent One. The name of my god could have a ring to it that is psychological, like "self-integration," or political, like "the universal brotherhood of man." Some people may worship at the shrine of a god whose name they are not aware of and never thought about. All those are players in the religion game who are concerned with that ultimate reality which can give meaning to their lives as a whole. This goal is still vague, to be sure. But it is precise enough to exclude those who believe in nothing at all, and neither see nor care about the sense and meaning of their lives.

Now to the motivation of the religion game. What makes the players play? The religious person feels that an individual has a potential to fulfill, a human potential. One becomes fully human only by reaching that absolute goal, or by realizing that ultimate reality. Until this enlightenment, fulfillment, final communion or happiness is achieved or realized, one falls short of that potential. As a human being, such a person is not yet complete. Somehow human life involves a task or process of transformation; the religious dimension of life consists precisely in treading this path of transformation toward the ultimate goal. In achieving the goal or realizing the ultimate reality, the meaning of the religious person's life is fulfilled and authenticated. One's humanity is complete. This is still very vague, of course. This transformation will be described in different ways—as salvation, enlightenment, release, conversion. In every case, however, one plays the religious game precisely because there is a felt need of transformation in order to become fully human. This distinguishes one from those who care not about the religion game; these latter have no motivation to play. For the unreligious person, human is human, period. It is not a problem, a task or an invitation. It is not something to realize. Nor would an unreligious person be concerned in Zenlike fashion with realizing that there is nothing to realize. At no level is such a one concerned with a comprehensive goal or a life meaning, but lives matter-of-factly on the conditioned surface of minute-to-minute desires, pleasures and pains. That is all there is. But unreligious people neither question nor affirm whether that is all. If they did, they would be in the religion game. And the religion game is to them a matter of indifference and irrelevance. They have no reason, no motive, for playing.

We hope, then, that this goal and motive is precise enough to distinguish the religion game from other human games, and the religious person from the unreligious. At the same time, we hope that the definition is general enough to include in its net all the various human ways of being religious. The goal is ultimate reality. The motive is transformation toward becoming fully human, which implies coming into some relationship with this ultimate reality. The third element of our working definition involves the various *means* of transformation, the various moves of the religion game.

These moves are the "how to" of religion. They would form the book of strategy and tactics. Granting the goal, and granting that you want to play, such a book would tell you how to go about playing. Again, at this stage we must remain vague about the moves. We confine ourselves in this preliminary definition to the statement that religion prescribes certain *means* to the goal. There are moves to make in the religion game. Religion, as a way of being human, affects the behaviors of my human life. Human activities and attitudes are involved. And these are specifically religious. They are defined by a religious goal, and acted upon because of religious motivation. It is this that sets them apart from nonreligious activities which may on the surface appear very similar to the religious. Mysticism, obedience, rituals, personal encounters, social programs, magic, acts of faith and commitment—each of these may qualify as a move in various religion games. Clearly, the same types of activities can be performed in nonreligious games. They must be judged in the light of the goal of religion, viz., ultimate reality, and in the light of religious motivation, viz., overall transformation. In such a context, they are moves in a genuinely religious game. Otherwise, the real game in which such moves are being made is something other than religious. Neurotic rituals can resemble religious ones, and the peace corps worker can look like the religious missionary. But if the goals and motivations are different, then the games are different. A psychological or patriotic game is not to be confused with a religious one, even though the moves appear the same on the surface.

To sum up briefly, we focus not on *religions,* but on human ways of being *religious.* We will be objective. But objectivity does not require us to deny our religious commitments and biases. We must rather consciously recognize them and take them into account. The game metaphor symbolizes this double attitude embracing both the *distance* we place between ourselves and religion and, at the same time, the *commitments* we have at stake as players of the game.

Our final introductory task was to come up with this working definition: the religion game embraces all those human activities and attitudes that have ultimate reality as their goal, and the achievement of full human potential as their motivation. Those who play this game are religious. Those who do not care to play are nonreligious.

*The Religion Game: American Style* is the double title of this book reflecting the two parts into which it is divided. Part One concerns the religion game in general. Here we will expound on the sociology of religious knowledge. Part Two focuses on "The American Style" of playing the religion game. Here we will sketch a philosophy of religion which peculiarly reflects the American temper and cast of thought. This has been a particularly neglected area. Much of our American religious experience seems out of joint because, whether we realize it or not, it is a foreign import. It has its origins in Greco-Roman civilization, medieval scholasticism, Anglo-European Reformation thought, modern British linguistic analysis or continental phenomenologico-existentialist philosophy. The result is that religion in America has been compartmentalized away from the mainstream of our day-to-day living experiences.

This schizophrenia is a pity. We will take a small step toward healing the rift. There are rich untapped sources in American philosophical thought which point the way for us. There is no reason why the religious dimension of human experience cannot embrace our empirical, pragmatic, freedom-loving tendencies. There is no reason why the religion game cannot be deeply rooted in *experience*, a word we hold so dear. This thirst for an experiential dimension to the religious has sent many Americans looking toward the orient. This affinity of America and the East is not a mere recent fad. To mention but two examples, John Dewey was being welcomed in Japan with open arms during the first quarter of this century, and in more recent decades American philosopher Van Meter Ames has pointed out and fostered the close harmony between Zen and American thought in his work at the East-West Center, a geographic and intellectual stepping stone located symbolically on the mid-Pacific Hawaiian Island of Oahu.

Part Two of this book will explore these themes of experience, freedom, and action, which characterize the American style of playing the religion game. Under the rubric of "Religious Experience" we will outline the foundations for an American philosophy of religion which have been laid by Charles Saunders Peirce, William James, John Dewey, and George Herbert Mead.

All of these writers speak in the tradition of pragmatism in America. Religion is not a luxury, but a pragmatic human need. Such is the angle we take toward "Religious Freedom." We are not concerned with civil liberties, but with religion as a pragmatic condition of human freedom.

But before taking up this American angle on religion, Part One looks at the religion game in general. In the first chapter we plunge right into the sociological origins of the religion game. The rather subversive sounding title of Chapter One says it all: "Religion in the

Reality-Construction Business." This calls for an explanation. We will see what it means.

One final disclaimer before launching into the deep. What follows is neither a treatise on the sociology of religious knowledge, nor a definitive statement of the American philosophy of religion. Rather, it is a somewhat loosely connected set of probes into religion. It is a record of some of the sparks and flashes illuminating religion when sociology and philosophy cross swords. The footnotes can lead you into the more scholarly treatments whenever you feel the need to fan the sparks into a more sustained and steadier flame.

# PART ONE
# THE RELIGION GAME

# ONE: RELIGION IN THE REALITY-CONSTRUCTION BUSINESS

Religion is in the reality-construction business. Of course, neither the original Christian Gospels nor any human religion was deliberately and consciously manufactured. We merely wish to suggest that what passes for religious knowledge represents less the "facts of life" than a "man-made cosmos." Does this mean that religious knowledge is somehow inferior to other types of knowledge? Is this the old science-versus-religion battle in which scientific facts win the day over religious myths? By no means.

*All human knowledge is mythological.* Religion deals in myths. Science deals in myths. Myth, as we are using the word here, does not mean fairy tale or fiction. By myth we mean an explanatory story. A myth is an explanation that tries to make sense out of the chaos of experience. Myths in science are usually called "theories." Myths in religion are usually called "theologies." Both types of knowledge are myth-making games. Human knowledge is the ongoing effort to tell ourselves stories which will give sense and coherence to our lives.

A recent California court decision, for example, declared evolution to be only a theory, not a fact. Television news commentators found this decision a source of great merriment. They implied that in this enlightened age, evolution should be considered an obvious fact. But the fact is that no self-respecting biologist would agree with them. Evolution is a theory, a hypothesis, a myth, which is revisable, and possibly some day disposable. It is the story which seems to make the most sense of the data now in our possession in the context of all the other credible myths that make up our contemporary body of scientific knowledge.

13

Once it was an obvious fact (read myth) that the earth was the center of the universe. In 1600, Giordano Bruno was burned at the stake for, among other things, suggesting an alternative heliocentric myth placing the sun at the center of the universe. Today, we are unconcerned about the universe's center, and prefer to think of the sun as a star at the edge of a galaxy. We have no way of knowing what stories about the universe our great-great-great-grandchildren will tell themselves.

In this perspective, American logician W. V. Quine calls the profoundest laws of astronomy or atomic physics a "man-made fabric." Or in the words of the German philosopher, Edmund Husserl, they are "experiences dressed in the cloth of ideas." The point of all this is that religion has no monopoly upon the world of myth. It is mythology that enables modern human beings to worship at the altar of science. So the religionists need not apologize for bringing mythology to their worship at the altar of God. In medieval and even in renaissance times, the privileged altar was religious. Scientific myths were made to bow before the religious altar—whence the sleepless nights suffered by Galileo Galilei. In modern times, the privileged altar is scientific. The tables are turned. It is science that demands an accounting from religion. Theologians stay up nights devising ways to make religious myths—papal infallibility, for example, or the image of a Creator Father God—pay their obeisance to science. Such are the vagaries of the shifting winds of culture.

Prevalent is the "enlightened" view that this shift from religious myths to scientific represents "progress." The sociologist of knowledge views the situation quite differently and, I might venture, more objectively.[1] Despite the inevitable de facto legislations of a given culture and era, no particular set of myths has the *right* to privileged treatment. Religion, of course, enjoyed privileged treatment in early renaissance times just as science enjoys it today. But objectively speaking, the web of human knowledge is a precarious human construction, and the decision to grant privileged status to a particular set of myths is, itself, the result of a social consensus rather than of an imposed objective reality.

This discarding of old myths in favor of new ones—isn't this progress? It is progress, if you like. The myth of progress is called "meliorism" which literally means "better-ism." Things are getting better and better all the time. New science is better science. New religion is better religion. Change is always for the best. But this is not the only way to look at the course of human history. You can adopt the pessimistic myth: science in the form of technology is smothering what is best in humanity. What was thought to be progress is being revealed as race suicide. The decline of the traditional forms of religion is only a symptom of this degeneration. The species is doomed. There is no ultimate hope on this globe. Either despair, or look for hope in another life. There is something radically destructive about the course of scientific and religious myths. American pragmatists like John Dewey had a great faith in the myth of progress as signalled by the "advance" of science and the decline of religious "superstitions." On the other hand, scientist Aldous Huxley was perfectly prepared to view the human race as a dying species, and there is no lack of religious prophets who for their own different reasons proclaim an equally gloomy prognosis.

Note that both the optimistic myth of progress and the pessimistic myth of decline are both touted under the banner of "what we *know*." The sociologist of knowledge, however, points out that "what we know" is dressed in mythological clothing. As the heading of this section states: *All human knowledge* (be it scientific or religious or other) *is mythological.* Neither scientific progress nor religious gloom need be accepted as privileged or superior knowledge. Each is an explanatory myth. Each is a story that believers tell themselves in order to make sense out of their lives. The same might be said for scientific gloom or religious hope. This view of human knowledge is not a counsel of skepticism. It is simply a warning not to take our own propaganda too seriously. The year 1976 is not necessarily witnessing the highest scientific and religious achievements in the history of mankind. It is not necessary to think that the year 2000 will be better. You will disagree, of course, if you have adopted for yourself the melioristic myth of human history; you will believe that things were in a worse state in 1900. And true believers in the pessimistic myth of human history will arrive at their contrary conclusions for contrary reasons. Each side, of course, has the right to believe as they do. And as people believe, so they will shape the course of their lives. The father of American pragmatism, William James, has analyzed this immense power of faith in his famous essay "The Will to Believe," as we will see later on. Such beliefs have quite the opposite effect from inducing despair or cynical skepticism, even when seen through the sociologist's penetrating eye. They form rather the very fabric of human knowledge.

The intent of the sociologist is not to undermine knowledge, but to see it for what it is. When we see through to its mythological character, we are able to construct more adequate myths if need be. Though the truth may hurt, it never fails to strengthen. The sociologist forces us to face what might be to some the unpalatable truth about our own truths, viz., their character as human constructions. Do not take your own perspective as the be-all and end-all, we are cautioned. Then you will be free to enter into other perspectives. As we will see later in the pragmatic philosophy of G. H. Mead, it is this ability to place ourselves in the other person's shoes that makes us human. Only the human animal, among all the species, can do this. Indeed in this very power lies our hope of achieving that universal human community which is the ideal of the great world religions, especially Christianity. This energy is released, once we see our myths for what they are, once we do not take too seriously our own propaganda. If I am not overly bewitched by the scientific and theological achievements of 1976, I become free to appreciate the thought achievements of generations past, and to look forward to the new constructions of generations to come. In the act of seeing through the new theologies of my own time, I become less the slave of contemporary fads and trends. While thoroughly contemporary in my outlook, I am able at the same time to embrace both traditionalism and futurism as part of my human perspective. And in appreciating the powerful force of religious mythologies other than my own, I am free both to enrich and draw strength from the mythological truth system which is the foundation of my own religious tradition.

This sociological point of view at first glance seems subversive, but in the end it is a liberation and a strength. In liberating me from the enslaving grip of the present it forces me to embrace both past and future. In freeing me from the narrow prison walls of my own individual perspective, it enables me to look at the universe through the eyes of every other person. Rigid dogmatists and inflexible liberals alike suffer their deepest agonies in times of religious change. The former become disillusioned when they see the mythological and transitory character of what they had thought were solid and eternal traditional truths, and so they "lose the faith." The latter are disillusioned when they see the variety of forms that contemporary truths take. They conclude that all religious truths were "mere myths," become skeptical and "lose the faith." Both fail to see that all human knowledge, be it scientific or theological, is mythological. It is the best knowledge we have, the human way of grasping and explaining truth. There is nothing shameful in the fact that human beings have always told themselves explanatory stories about their experience, and that they will always continue to do so. Such is the human condition. In accepting the relativity of our stories about the universe (science) and about religion and God (theology), we can draw from these stories the strength and meaning they are intended to give. In telling it like it is, the sociologist does not undermine our knowledge but liberates us to draw strength from it in the best possible human ways.

All right, you say, humans are myth-makers. They tell themselves explanatory stories about the world, dub them as truths, and live their lives by them. Isn't this sociological explanation of knowledge also a myth, an explanatory story which the sociologist asserts to be the true explanation of the nature of knowledge? Every myth-maker has his/her own assumptions about the way the world and/or God really is. In other words, every myth-maker has his/her own philosophy. It is time to lay our philosophical cards on the table so that you can take a preliminary peek at them. The philosophical backdrop is American pragmatism. That is the import of analyzing the religion game *American style.* Hopefully this will become clearer as you read through the whole book which states an American philosophy of religion. Here we will only give a preliminary clue by facing some very basic questions: Is one scientific explanation as good as another? Is one religion as good as another? Isn't there any difference between reality and illusion? What makes me say that one scientific explanation is more real and true than another? What makes me think that one religion is more real and true than another? Does the history of human religious knowledge form a supermarket of myths which differ only in their brand names? Does it make any difference which religious myths I pick to live my life by, and which ones I choose to leave on the shelf unbought?

Tough questions. Let us start off by saying that we make no assumptions about whether our myths, either scientific or religious, are getting better and better or worse and worse. One thing is clear. Our myths, both scientific and religious, certainly do change. Whether the change is for the better or not, the fact remains that the truths of yesterday are not always acceptable for today. In religion as in science, change comes slowly, reluctantly, painfully. But change we must. Why? The sociologist of knowledge describes, gives a movie of, the process of how men *do* change their myths. The philosopher asks *why.* What is there about reality and human experience which forces us to act the way we do? Why are we myth-making animals? And what makes us change and modify our myths?

The answer is not simple, but it can be stated briefly: our myths or truths are neither completely arbitrary and subjective nor completely necessary and objective. They are a combination of both poles. As the Chinese would say, everything is a combination of polar opposites, of *yin* and *yang*. When I say "reality" I am looking toward the objective pole, "the facts." When I say "experience" I am looking to the subjective pole, "the myths." But neither in science nor in religion are there any such things as "brute facts." Neither in science nor in religion are there any such things as "arbitrary myths." Facts are always seen through mythological eyeglasses. The combination, I call truth. Myths are always clothed in facts. This makes one declare them true. The mind does not invent its myths in a vacuum. Both science and religion have to pass the test of reality, of real life. On the other hand, the facts of life do not dictate our myths, our various *ways of looking at* the facts. True knowledge is the happy marriage of myths and facts, or experience and reality. Anyone who knows anything about science has long ago abandoned the absurd prejudice that science just "reports the facts," but that same absurd prejudicial objection against religion has not died. Humankind's religious truths are dismissed as mere fairy tales because they are not based upon hard empirical facts in the way that scientific theory is supposedly based. The same kind of truth game is going on in both science and religion. And in its delicate effort to balance reality and experience, the objective and the subjective, reason and faith, facts and values (put it any way you want), religion need make no apologies to science.

So this book intends to be more than a sociological description of how people play the religion game. It is an inquiry into the philosophical truth about the religion game. And our inquiry has a distinctively American flavor: religion will be shown to have strong respectable roots in human experience.

*The Name of the Game.* Possibly the one thing most universally true about the human experience of reality is that nothing is universally true about it. Human speech does not divide itself into sounds, words, and languages. Language games are human inventions. I grew up, of course, taking it for granted that English was the only proper way to speak. And even today when I speak another language I feel as though I'm only *playing* at speaking. It is in English alone that I *really* speak. Even though I know better, I marvel at how three-year-old Japanese children can be so fluent in Japanese. The English language to me is part of my taken-for-granted world. It is something that "everybody knows." It shapes the way I think, see, hear, and experience my universe. In fact, we who conspire to play the English language game thereby experience a different world from the one created by the players of the Japanese language game. Experience does not interpret itself. The human mind imposes meanings upon it. And the language game is one of the most fundamental ways we create the world we act and live in. Do you begin to see some possible parallels in the human religion game?

Before touching on religion, let us move to another area of human experience, viz., morality. Like my language, so also are my morals a human creation. Human behavior does not divide itself up into moral good and moral evil. Morality games are human inventions. I grew up, of course, in a world in which adultery, masturbation, human sacrifice, and stealing are moral evils, and in which monogamy, meat-eating and private property are moral goods. In my taken-for-granted world, various types of human behavior come stamped with ready-made moral labels. And even today, although my mind understands the rationale behind Eskimo wife-swapping, my moral sensibility would not be at ease with the practice, and even though I understand the reason for the Hindu moral taboo against beef-eating, I *feel* that their moral revulsion for the practice is exaggerated. My values, to me, are part of my taken-for-granted world. They are something "everybody knows." These values shape the way I think, see, hear and act. Those who have seduced me into playing this morals game have created for me a world that is different from that which is experienced and lived in by the players of the Hindu morals game. Human behavior does not interpret itself. The human mind imposes values upon it. And after language, the morals game is one of the most fundamental ways by which we create the world we act and live in. From this perspective on science, language and morals, do you get an idea of how the sociologist will view the religion game?

Are we doomed to complete relativism? Is one language as good as another? Is one morality game as good as another? Is one scientific theory as good as another? Is one religion as good as another? Certainly, the appearance of relativism is here. This is because we have been stressing the subjective creative side of human experience. But as we indicated above, reality has an objective pole as well. We cannot create our myths out of whole cloth. And although our games are human inventions, we cannot arbitrarily fool around with either our choice of games or with the rules. Whether we are talking about the language game, the morals game, the science game, or the religion game, some games *are* better than others. The human ability to create reality is not limitless or without its controls. The bipolar character of the human experience of reality cannot be ignored with impunity. Subjective behavior is conditioned by the objective environment in which it occurs. My *experience* has to come to terms with the very *reality* it would shape to its own purposes. I have *values* but their realization must give way to *facts*. In other words, while it is true that reason is born of faith (the mythological side of human knowledge), it is no less true that faith must bow to reason. Faith unchecked by reason is madness: in science, it turns chemistry into alchemy, and astronomy into astrology; in ethics, it spawns moralistic utopias, and religion becomes superstition. So whether we are talking about science, morality or religion, it is not true to say that one myth is as good as another.

How discern true myth from false? How tell the better from the worse? No long argument is necessary, says the pragmatist. Outworn myths that are false to human experience will die a natural death. The true and better myths are those which foster human life and help us to evolve and grow. They are true to the extent that they pass the acid test of action. There was a time, for example, when the scientific myth of a flat earth served human purposes very well. And though there is a Flat Earth Society today, its membership is not burgeoning. The global traveler today would stay home if he or she feared falling off the earth's edge. And even the homebody would find the flat earth myth inadequate for an understanding of what one sees on TV or reads in books.

The taboo against killing fellow humans is a moral myth that has served well the survival and growth of the human species. But the subjective definition or myth about who is human and who is not shifts according to the demands of the objective environment in which human action is tested and controlled. There are Indian tribes in Latin America where the harsh facts of a high infant mortality rate and a need for population control are made comprehensible by the myth of not certifying the infant as human until it has survived for a year outside the womb. Only then is its birth registered and does it receive an official name. In the Ecuadorian Andes, for example, during the months after birth, the infant is designated by the sexless appellation *guagua* (onomatopoetically pronounced "whah-whah"). Since it is likely to die, the family can ill afford the kind of heavy investment of emotions and expectations that American parents lavish on their newborn. And if it dies, there is a shrug of the shoulders: "it was only a *guagua*." The event has the emotional significance that an early miscarriage would here in America. There can be no successful wars unless we can succeed in defining the enemy as somehow less than human. Soldiers' language inevitably creates a "devil" myth of the enemy, thus enabling the soldier to avoid violating the moral taboo against killing one's own kind. The abortion debate in America is at bottom a process of defining which is the truer and better myth about the humanity of the foetus.

Neither can religious myths escape the survival test of daily human living and experience. A religious myth which is totally directed away from and irrelevant to human experience will wither and die. But no more than scientific or moral myths are our religious myths subject to purely objective proof. In science, morality and religion, it is my subjective purposes that guide my actions. Purposes and plans are not given to me by experience. They are the result of decisions, acts of faith, desires and choices. But my purposes are vitally realized only to the extent that they mesh with objective experience. Religion rests on my act of faith in my overall purpose in life. But religious faith divorced from daily living experience becomes empty and dead. So to demand that religious myths meet the survival test of experience is not to deny the role of faith. Faith and reason go hand in hand in religion, as they do in science and morality. As Nietzsche cynically observed, it takes a strong faith indeed to indulge in the luxury of skepticism. To throw away the test of experience in religion is to throw away faith as well. We will be returning to these themes in ever greater depth.

So philosophically speaking, the question "Do you believe in craters on the planet Mercury?" or the question "Do you believe in incest?" is not all that different from the question "Do you believe in God?" The truth or falsity of each belief depends both on a subjective act of faith and an objective relevance to living experience. The main thrust of this book is to show that this is the case, though at this point the parallel may seem outrageous. We do not hesitate to use our reason and experience to test our beliefs about the moon, but we hesitate to subject our moral beliefs to the test of experience: Pope Paul VI rejected the findings of his own commission on birth control just as President Nixon rejected the conclusions of his own committee on the effects of pornography. And if we hesitate to philosophically test our moral beliefs, then inquiry into religious beliefs can seem to be outright blasphemy. But in the religion game American style (i.e., as viewed by the pragmatist), such inquiry into religion is the path not to blasphemy but to living faith—whence comes the inspiration for this book.

To sum up, then, we do not claim that one religion is as good as another. All human knowledge rests both on a subjective act of faith, and an objective testing in experience. Philosophically speaking, the question "Do you believe in craters on the planet Neptune?" or the question "Do you believe in incest?" is not all that different from the question "Do you believe in God?" The Neptune question rests on an act of faith in a certain model of the universe, where planets are different from stars, where certain configurations are called "craters," and craters are worth worrying about. The God question also assumes an act of faith in a possible model of the universe, where there is more to human life than minute-to-minute survival, and that my transformation in terms of such an ultimate reality might be worth my concern.

We cannot, however, stop here. What makes one myth, one religion, better or truer than another? They must pass the survival test. Scientific, ethical, and religious acts of faith will survive only if they pass the test of objective human experience. Our myths are not arbitrary creations. It made experiential sense for Thomas Aquinas to view "Neptune" as an angel; 1000 years hence it might be a mining outpost for Earth; now it is a planet. The survival of a static tribal society may depend on an incest myth where marriage of third cousins is a crime. In highly mobile America, genetic survival requires no such myth. Similarly, the growth and death of theistic or atheistic myths depend on their ability to integrate and foster living human experience. All human knowledge rests both on a subjective act of faith and an objective testing in experience. So I ask myself the personal question: what does the religious dimension of this experience reveal to me? What does my experience reveal to me about my myth? What is my game?

# TWO: RELIGIOUS MYTH AS GIVER OF MEANING

*Whether the world is intimate or impersonal, lawful or magical depends on your perspective. World views are like glasses. They can be steel gray, rosy, or black and white. In the matter of cosmic sight, we all wear some kind of lenses.*

*Sam Keen and Anne Valley Fox*, Telling Your Story[1]

*Meaning is wider in scope as well as more precious in value than is truth.*

*John Dewey*, Philosophy and Civilization[2]

*I would conclude that interpretive beliefs are brought to religious experience as much as they are derived from it. There is a greater influence in religion than in science 'from the top down': from paradigms, through interpretive models and beliefs, to experience. But the influence 'from the bottom up,' starting from experience, is not totally absent in religion. Although there is no neutral descriptive language, there are degrees of interpretation. Therefore, religious beliefs, and even paradigms, are not totally incommensurable. There can be significant communication between paradigm communities. One cannot prove one's most fundamental beliefs, but one can try to show how they function in the interpretation of experience.*

*Ian Barbour*, Myths, Models, and Paradigms[3]

It is hard to be neutral in the face of religious myths.[4] They challenge me to take a stand, for or against. It is the lukewarm, the wishy-washy, said Jesus, whom God vomits from his mouth. The temptation of the true believer is to treat religious myths with kid gloves. They are privileged and untouchable. They transcend time and history. They are an abiding source of permanence and order in a world that is otherwise in flux, change and confusion. They are the true account of humanity's dealings with the Absolute Transcendent Divinity. The unbeliever has an equal and opposite temptation to puncture religious myths as pretentious in their claims and ridiculous in their failures, pointing out absurdities in the myths themselves and contradictions among myths, as well as their incongruities with science and common sense. The unbeliever is tempted to discard the whole religious enterprise as trivial and unworthy.

Pragmatism would want neither to absolutize religious myths nor to trivialize them. There is a middle ground. On the one hand, against the absolutists, religions and their myths are historically rooted and culturally conditioned. Far from affording a springboard out of the historical process, they are infected with all the messiness that is part and parcel of this human world of change and fallibility. Whatever is bizarre, confused, and contradictory about people will not be absent from their religions. On the other hand, pragmatism stands against those who would trivialize religious myths or abandon the religious enterprise. Religion is, or can be, a powerful cultural force. It deserves to be examined for what it *actually does.*

*Pragma,* in Greek, means action. Pragmatism, then, is a philosophy of action.[5] If you want to know what a thing is, see how it acts. This advice is no recent invention. Thomas Aquinas himself enunciated such a principle in the thirteenth century: *agere sequitur esse* ("as a thing is, so it acts"). You are what you do. A myth is what a myth does. What do religious myths *do* for me? What is the function of religious myths?

We have here a handle for getting a hold of that elusive human phenomenon of religion. In the pragmatic view, there is no specifiable difference between religion and the role it plays in civilization. To examine, abolish, or revamp religion and its myths means to examine, abolish, or revamp the *function* of religion and its myths. If religion is dying, its function is dying. If religion would be reborn, its function must be reborn. So first of all let us be clear about just what it is that religious myths do.

We distinguish two main functions of religious myths. They give *meaning* to our individual lives, to the community of believers, and to the world. And they tell us *truths* about our individual lives, about the community and about the world. Following the lead of John Dewey (see quotation at the head of this chapter) I will stress the meaning-giving function of religious myths as far more precious and important than their truth-giving function. The question of truth is sometimes not without importance; we will examine it in the next chapter. But if you would appreciate the full richness of the role that religion plays, you will look first to the meaning it gives to human life. You can miss the whole point if you jump right off to questions like, How do you prove the existence of God? or, Is Christianity true? In fact, questions of *truth* often are not even relevant, and it is wrong-headed to persist in asking them. To ask, Is Christianity true? is in a way as silly and muddle-headed as to ask, Is Greek civilization true? The question just does not fit.

The pertinent question about Greek civilization or Christianity, or Buddhism, or Hinduism, concerns meaning, not truth. I look first to the meanings enshrined in religious myths. What values are enshrined for me in the story of Christ's life, death, and resurrection? What ideals are held out to the devout Hindu by Krishna's teaching and actions in the *Gita*? I miss the point if my main preoccupation is to determine which is the true incarnation, Krishna's or Christ's. Far more to the point is it to determine the meanings given by the Krishna story and the Christ story to the Hindu and Christian communities.

It is the role of scientific myths to introduce meaning into the raw data of observation. Similarly, says Dr. Ian Barbour (a professor of religion as well as of physics), it is the role of religious myths to suggest beliefs that will introduce meaning into certain broad areas of human experience.[6] The specifically religious domain of experience is that by which I orient my life as a whole. The presence of this sense of overall personal meaning, or at least concern about such a meaning, is the distinguishing mark of the religious as opposed to the unreligious. For the unreligious, simply unreflective day-to-day survival is enough. Such people do not even wonder whether it is enough or not. Their lives remain fragmented without unified pattern or orientation. The function of religious myth is to introduce into my life such overall pattern and meaning as are lacking in the life of the unreligious.

Different types of human experience give rise to the concern for ultimate meaning. Correspondingly, religious myths function in distinctive ways to satisfy this concern. I am enabled to place and interpret experiences that otherwise would remain raw and senseless. Let us look specifically at some of these different domains of human experience, and see how religious myth functions to give them meaning.

The first function of religious myth is to make sense out of the experience of mystery, wonder, awe in the face of the Other. This is what Rudolf Otto calls the experience of the sacred in which fascination and dread are combined.[7] Correlative to this is the sense of my own limitations and dependence, and the unavoidable certainty of my own mortality. This raw experience cries out for interpretation. I need to tell myself a story in order to make sense out of the fact that I am sure to die, that I am utterly dependent, utterly limited. In the face of such dread experience I need a myth to live by.

Of course, if I have never experienced the sacred, never been overwhelmed by a sense of awe, never thought of my own dying and my own limitations, then I need no story to make sense of such things. But most of us cannot forever avoid thinking about the fact of death. Most of us at least on occasion reflect on the immensity of the world, the life force, the stars, the universe, the course of evolution before which our individual lives seem to pale into insignificance. Note the word *in*significance, lack of significance, lack of meaning. This meaning-void is what I must fill. Religion's first function is to tell me the story that fills this void.[8]

Many are the stories that are told about death. This is not the place to review them. Some are stories of stoicism or of despair that call death an ending. There are stories of hope where death is called a rebirth and beginning. The significance of my life will shift radically depending upon which story I make my own. Note that what is primarily at stake here is meaning rather than truth, a meaningful myth to live by rather than a true story.

Many are the stories that are told about that Other before which I bow. It is God. It is Brahman. It is the Evolutionary Life Force. It is an impersonal swirl of atoms. My life will take on a different significance depending on which myth I live by. The truth of my myth is not irrelevant (in the next chapter we examine the truth-question), but its meaning for my life encompasses so much more than truth. My myth is a story of values, ideals, goals, origins, feelings, as well as truths. This whole rich complexus goes into the significance-conferring function of religious myth. It tells me who I am, gives me a place in the sun.

The fundamental myths that I live by stand in judgment of all the others. It is these basic myths that are the religious ones. They do not always *sound* religious. You won't know the religion of Mary Jones until you learn which of her myths comes first in her life. Which one will she hold on to at all costs, even at the price of sacrificing the others? Would she sacrifice her part-time job for her family? Would she give up her family for God? Would she give up her Catholicism for the freedom to find and develop herself authentically as Mary Jones? If the myth "I am Mary Jones" comes first, then her religion is one aimed at achieving authenticity and self-integration. This is the ultimate reality that gives overall meaning to her life. The "Other" that she worships she finds in the depth of her own self. This is how, for her, religious myth fulfills its first function. According to Mary Jones's story, her own authentically developing self is the being before whom she ultimately stands in awe.[9]

A second function of religious myth is the role it plays in my moral life. The experience of moral obligation will take on different meanings according to the religious myth I use to pattern and interpret this experience. Of course there can be morality without religion, especially without traditional religion. Indeed many people abandon traditional religion precisely because it detracts from responsible adult moral decision-making. And there is no doubt that religious myth can function in an infantile way. Both popular Christianity and popular Hinduism, for example, have religious myths about angry gods and fiery hells to frighten children and others into walking the moral straight and narrow path. But religious myth can direct my moral life along less childish paths. Religious myth can build up community by portraying God as moral lawgiver. Thus the moral values which are precious to the community are enshrined in a mythic statement to which all can give allegiance. The commandments issued on Sinai, for example, were a moral charter protecting the marital, ecclesiastical, judicial, and property structures so necessary for the survival of the Hebrew people.

Religious myth, however, can cast my moral life into a pattern of meaning that is even more mature and more autonomous. In the 1960s, for example, many Christian moralists abandoned the myth of God the lawgiver. They told a new story about the moral life and its relationship to God. Christians were no longer to consider themselves as children obedient to a father in heaven. Humankind had come of age, as theologian Bonhoeffer said. Responsibility for moral decision-making was to shift from heaven to earth. No more moral bulletins could be expected from on high. The function of this new religious myth was to make humans aware of the weight of responsibility they carried for their moral lives, and to set them free to act accordingly. God was still to be in the picture, but in a fresh and liberating way. Religious myth need not function as a moral crutch. It can enhance moral autonomy and adult freedom.

Myths have a third function. They help me to deal with the experience of moral failure, and the attendant guilt and anxiety. How often I perversely act against my conscience. I am unfaithful to my own best lights. I betray friendships. I hurt others and I hurt myself. And I have to live with the sense of guilt that such actions arouse. There is evil in myself and I do not know how to accept it. I have done evil, and I do not know how to undo the harm. Guilt unresolved can lead to anxiety and to self-destructive masochism.

The third function of religious myth is to help me make sense of this experience of guilt and moral failure. Without a religious myth to sustain me, this sense of emptiness, defect, ignorance, sin—call it what you will—can lead to despair, or at best to gnawing quiet desperation. This insight is the burden of contemporary psychiatrist Karl Menninger's recent book, *What Ever Became of Sin?* [10] In the morass of personal weakness, man's cruelty to man, suffering and nameless anxiety, where is hope to be found? Menninger gives a psychiatrically unorthodox but old-fashioned answer to that incessant malaise that plagues us all. Hope is what you want? In religion is where you will find it, he says. Just make sure that you properly diagnose your sinful condition.

The loss of a sense of sin, says Menninger, happened in two stages. The first stage is a result of the good old American penchant for confusing law and morality. Sins became crimes. We like to see our morality written in the lawbooks. There was a shift from personal responsibility for sin to the more impersonal determinations of illegality—crime. In stage two, crimes ceased to be crimes, and became illnesses. The criminal is not personally guilty, but is "sick." This confusion of sin with sickness is disastrous, in Menninger's view.

> It does little good to repent a symptom, but it may do great harm not to repent a sin. Vice versa, it does little good merely to psychoanalyze a sin, and sometimes a great harm to ignore a symptom. [11]

Religion restores a sense of sin, and with it, hope. I must return to a courageous facing of my responsibility for evil. My hope lies in my own hands, and not in a plaintive cry of "Doctor, cure me." I do not look with optimism to the courts or prisons for the reformation of evil. Evil there is, and it is only the evil-doer who can undo the evil he or she has done. As the Buddha said, "Each person is responsible for working out his own salvation." There is no other savior. Christianity has a different myth, but the same stress on responsibility. There is a savior—Jesus. But the onus is on me to accept responsibility for evil, atone for it, and accept the freely offered grace of forgiveness.

Religion without responsibility degenerates into magic. This third function of religious myth is to tell people the story of the hope of salvation. Religious myths, then, have a saving power. They picture humanity's ideal state. They tell us how and why we fall short. And they point out to us the path of transformation. They make available the power to overcome our basic flaw so that we can reestablish ourselves in the ideal kingdom. Various religions tap different sources for this saving power. It can come in personal form—a redeemer. It may be embodied in ritual acts, in a moral code, or in a discipline for living. The religion game is involved more in the transformation of life than in its explanation. This brings us to religious myth's fourth function which is likewise eminently practical.

This fourth function of religious myth has, like the third, a dynamic bearing on action. It is also very much an expansion of the first chapter's theme: religion in the reality-construction business. Religious myth has the role of ordering human experience and thereby providing concrete patterns for human action. Religious myth provides the context, the guide, and the legitimation for the ways that human beings pattern their political lives, their family lives and their sexual lives. Further, it makes sense out of those marginal areas of experience, like evil and death, where meaning threatens to dissolve into chaos. Let us dwell for a moment on religion's role in providing concrete patterns for human action.

Again, this function of religion responds to a deep human need. Human community would be utterly impossible outside of such a web of meaning as religious myth provides. This need for a socially contrived structure in which to operate sets the human species apart from the lower animal species. The lower species have no such need. The patterns of significant activity for the horse, the giraffe and the earthworm, for example, are biologically determined and species-specific. The patterns of equine sex do not vary from culture to culture. Giraffes everywhere feed from the tops of trees. And in garden after garden earthworms do their earthworm work according to the invariant rhythms and patterns of the earthworm species. The political life of African elephants is perfectly predictable wherever the species is found. The herding instinct and the biologically structured fights for flock leadership tell the whole story. The family life of antarctic penguins is biologically determined and likewise invariant. Mother penguin lays the egg, father penguin hatches it. No sexual liberation movements are in the offing here! The workings of paternal and maternal penguin instincts provide sufficient structure for family life without further addition. And finally, biology tells the whole story of animal sexual behavior. Dogs need no *Kama Sutra* or sex manuals. The position is *a tergo,* and the time is when the bitch is in heat.

The human species, on the other hand, has not inherited such fixed specific patterns of herding, nursing, and sex. Humans, in other words, are not species-specific in their behavior, but world-open. Like other animals, humans have a herding instinct, an urge toward community. But having said this, it is still an open question how this instinct toward community will express itself. For humans, political structures do vary from culture to culture. Politically, humans are world-open, not species-specific. Human society needs some guide beyond instinct by which to pattern itself. Religious myth can supply such a pattern. Like other animals, humans have a nursing instinct, a biologically based impulse toward family life. But having said this, it remains an open question how this instinct toward family will shape itself. Kinship charts and family sexual roles vary widely from culture to culture. Human family structures are no less world-open than are human political structures, and no less in need of some guiding pattern beyond instinct alone. Religious myth can furnish such concrete pattern and structure. Finally, there is no need to elaborate on the world-open character of human sexual behavior. Humans have traditionally looked toward religious myth to provide orientation, meaning, and limitation to their sexual living, while defining as perversion and promiscuity such behavior as operates outside the myth.

In short, religious myth in this fourth function is what makes community possible. These mythologically based patterns of action are social in their origin and in their expression. They are the grounding for what counts as reality (religion in the reality-construction business) and as sanity. Philip Slater put it this way: "If many people share a symbol system, it is a culture; if only one does, it is a psychosis."[12] Even my uniqueness is a social product, unrecognizable outside of community.

Let us see briefly how religious myth functions in patterning human political behavior in America, yes, in secular materialistic America with its jealously guarded separation of church and state. Sociologist Robert Bellah has dubbed this religious patterning of American political experience "civil religion," borrowing the phrase from Rousseau.[13] American civil religion transcends all particular denominations. It is neither Christian nor Jewish. But the shared faith in the mythology of this religion profoundly shapes the way that Americans view their political structure and destiny. This religion's set of beliefs has been articulated by our leaders throughout history from the founding fathers even to leaders of today.

From the time of the Declaration of Independence until the Civil War, the images of the American religious myth were drawn from the Biblical experience of Israel. Beginning with the Civil War, Christian images were borrowed to articulate the American experience. In neither case was there any sectarian implication.

The Declaration of Independence and the Constitution could be viewed as the sacred scriptures of this civil religion. In the Declaration, the legitimacy of the new American nation was justified by appeal to a natural divine law higher than any human law. This divine law conferred upon men certain inalienable rights. That same Declaration appeals to God as judge of the republic's legitimacy and to God's protective providence over it. The motto on our coins "In God we trust" attests that this religious mythology by which we understand ourselves as a nation persists to this very day. Even the will of the people is subject to the higher criterion of divine judgment. The speeches of the presidents and political leaders during the first century of America's history focus on the Revolution as the key saving event. The Revolution was conceived as the new exodus of a chosen people from tyranny to freedom. Washington was the Moses appointed by God to lead this chosen people.

The Civil War evoked a new symbolism in the American civil religion. That tragic event introduced the theme of sacrifice and of rebirth from death. Lincoln at once articulated this new theme, and, in his own "martyr's" death, exemplified it. The theme of sacrifice endures even today. It helped legitimate our wars, as we will see, and helped us come to terms with ourselves as a nation when torn by the tragedies of the "martyred" Kennedys and Martin Luther King.

The two themes, then, of (1) Americans the chosen people specially favored by God (2) who are destined to bring about the birth of freedom through death and sacrifice join to form a powerful symbol system. This system, albeit operating below the level of consciousness for the most part, constructs for us on the gut level the reality that we understand as our American national community. It concretizes our ideals and mobilizes our energies. The power of religious myth to shape what we count as reality itself is not to be underestimated. Perhaps that power stands out most starkly when we see it abused. "America, a divinely chosen people, destined to suffer and if need be die in order to bring freedom to all peoples"—this religious myth is no empty rhetoric. It was such "rhetoric" that mobilized billions of dollars and the thousands upon millions of lives sacrificed to bring freedom to Southeast Asia. And the accents of this religious myth sound loud and clear in the bicentennial celebrations of America's role in the world today. Such is one small example of the fourth function of religious myth, viz., to construct community by serving as a concrete pattern of human action in the political sphere. Thus the world-open herding instinct of United States inhabitants is shaped into that very specific kind of community we know as America.

One could go on and give examples of how religious myth specifies the biologically world-open human instincts of nursing and of sex. Religion-and-family deserve to be spoken of in the same breath as God-and-country. And how often sexual morality is discussed in a climate of appeal to either the duty of obeying God-given laws or the right to enjoy God-given pleasures. One might question whether the community-building function of religious myth is as strong today as it was in the past. There is no doubt that the myths are changing in the face of new pressures and conflicts. Indeed one purpose of this book is to remythologize religion in a language that might be more congenial to American ears.

Religious myth need not always function conservatively by legitimating established patterns of action. A remythologized religion may indeed subvert the established reality. When the traditional myth breaks down, such "subversion" may be the only way to survive. In either case, religious myth's patterning and ordering function defends us against the chaos of infinite world-open possibility by narrowing our choices and pointing out a definite path to walk for the successful art of living.

We have delayed on this fourth function of religion because it is here that religion bears most upon action. The full implications of this pragmatic approach to religion will be developed in Part Two when we move into the "American Style" of playing the religion game. Suffice it to say here that we do not consider religion to be a luxury for human living. Religion finds its justification in the heart of human experience and action, or not at all. In this view, a religion divorced from human life is a travesty of the genuine article. We rightly demand of religion, "What have you done for me lately?" Religion is as religion does. We have seen four functions performed by religion in the service of human living. We move now to a fifth function which also bears on human action—*ritual* human action.

Religious myths are more than mental stories. Myths get acted out in rituals. Religious rites have fallen on hard times. We hear expressions like "empty rituals" and "mere formalized religion." Empty ritual is contrasted with down-to-earth everyday action which presumably is not empty, but rich and full: "Down with the sterile formalized religion of the Churches! Back to the individual in solitary mystical communion with nature!" Implicit in such sentiments is that ritual action is hollow, empty, and less than fully human, and that religious rites, far from serving human experience, do it a disservice. Is this really the case? Let us apply the test of action. Ritual is what ritual does. What does religious ritual do for me? The answer to this question will give us the fifth function of religious myth, viz., the power I receive by reenacting it in ritual.

Two sorts of people deprecate the role of ritual in their lives: the very "practical" and the very "mystical," and both are the worse for it. Impoverished ritual means impoverished life. The practical people lose out on *ideals*;[14] the mystical people lose out on *community*.[15] Each group is in its own way reduced to one-dimensional living. The power of religious ritual lies in its challenge to such easy one-eyed views. To successfully "do my own thing" I have to go beyond the boundaries of my individual self. In each case it is ritual that shows the way.

First, to be truly pragmatic, I have to be more than merely practical. Day-to-day compromise with evil is practical, and of course, necessary. But there is more to reality than the good and evil which happen to exist at the moment. Marxist philosopher Herbert Marcuse dramatically puts it this way: "That which is," he says, "cannot be true."[16] *That which is* is only part of the picture. "The harsh facts of life" need to be complemented by *ideals*. "That which is" needs to be complemented by "that which can and should be." And I am a poor human being indeed if I live only according to "the facts" and close my eyes to "possibilities," to goals and ideals that, although they do not exist now, can shape and pattern my action now to bring about the world I would like to see. World hunger, war, political corruption: these are all facts. I have to live with them. But the complete person also has to live with ideals: a world without hunger, peace among nations, and integrity in government. These ideals, not less than "the facts," are guides in our daily decisions. Facts and ideals together make up what is real and true.

Well, how do I integrate such ideals into my daily action if I cannot act on them? How do I bring the pie in the sky down onto the table of everyday living? What I cannot act on *practically*, I act out *ritually*. This is how humans keep their ideals alive for that day when they can make them a reality. I act out my ideals in rituals. Family peace and unity is an impossible ideal. But on Thanksgiving Day the family members declare a truce and, in the annual ritual around the dinner table, act as the one big happy family they would like to be, but are not. Thanksgiving Day dinner is one ritual by which that ideal is kept alive. We in the Western world have an ideal of Eastern Europe freed from Soviet control. We dare not make this ideal a practical reality by attempting war. So we turn to ritual. Each year we celebrate Captive Nations Week, thus keeping the ideal alive. We act out ritually that which we cannot accomplish practically.

This is one of the great services of religious ritual. It enriches my human life by enabling me to act out the ideals which are precious to me. I do not become resigned to things as they are. I keep my ideals alive. These ideals are reenforced by my action, albeit this action is in the "artificial" world of ritual rather than the practical world of everyday. Their impact is not artificial, but very real. Christians, for example, at the Eucharist, eat, drink and sing together. Strangers outside of church, inside they pray for and greet one another. In this way they ritually act out and keep vivid for themselves the Christian ideal of brotherhood. The story of Christ, the universal savior, offering his body and blood for all humanity, becomes more than a story. By ritual reenactment, the myth becomes an event in which I actually take part. I rise above the "practical" world where people hate, cheat, and fight wars. For a brief space I am able to actually live in my ideal world of love and understanding. In this way, religious ritual is not empty and divorced from human life, but rather serves to enrich it.

Ritual performs another service for me, and a paradoxical one at that. By conferring structure, it brings freedom. It is a corrective now not to excessive pragmatism but to excessive mysticism. Withdrawal from religious and social structures in the name of direct individual experience of the divine is not the path to freedom. Ritual is a corrective to such an error. It delivers me from the void of undefined potential. Recall that the human species is world-open. Without structure, I would not have the faintest idea how to act. I would flail about aimlessly in an infinite no-man's-land attempting to "do my own thing," an attempt doomed to fail because I do not know who or where I am. Through ritual, I shift my center of gravity to trans-individual purposes and forces. Ritual tells me what family I belong to, what caste, what profession. And by so defining me, it paradoxically expands the scope of my action. It takes me out of myself. I live for what is more than me, and thereby become more than I thought I could be.

To take the oath of office, for example, seems to be a ritual of submission and constriction. But many a person in the service of such an oath has grown and contributed in ways never dreamed of. In a similar way, in the ritual exchange of marriage vows I focus my commitment very concretely and specifically on one other person. The exclusiveness of such a contract might seem to diminish freedom. But in summoning my energies to the service of a goal outside myself, the ritual can help me grow in a way not possible to one who "freely" floats from love to love but never makes an emotional investment beyond the self. Diffused and structureless action is no pathway to freedom. And so rituals like baptism, Bar Mitzvah, or even the singing of the national anthem can serve as catalysts for growth and freedom. Their catalytic force comes paradoxically by restricting alternatives, defining identity, and thereby bringing energies into focus on a cause which lies beyond the individual self alone. My actions which were written in lower case letters are translated through ritual into capitals. I act but now not I: Christ acts in me (baptismal ritual), or the nation acts in me (patriotic rites), or my race acts in me (Bar Mitzvah rite). Japanese *haiku* poetic form narrowly restricts the poet to seventeen syllables. The resultant literature witnesses how the deepset feeling and highest spontaneity can be concentrated in this tight form. In similar fashion, religious ritual enables me to condense and focus my energies without losing any of my uniqueness and spontaneity. I can act with freedom and total commitment once I know who and where I am. And the loss of this service is the human price exacted by the decline of organized religion with its rituals.

Note that ritual operates on me in a nonrational way. In fact, the effort to be clear about rituals can diminish their impact. Rites are actions, not thoughts. They involve the whole person, especially on the unconscious affective level. At the Bar Mitzvah, the father's proud smile, the women's tears, and the nervous concentration in the young boy's voice—these need no theology to explain them. Something more than the merely rational is going on here. It is like the reply given to a Western guest at a Shinto ceremony. "What ideology lies behind these rites?" the guest had asked. "Oh, we don't have any ideology," his Japanese host replied, "we just dance." Religious ritual is a dance in which the mind plays the least important part. The decline of Western Christianity is perhaps due in no small part to the effort to be rational and clear. A religion demythologized and deritualized becomes impotent. The vernacular makes everything all too clear. The mind says, "Is that all there is? This doesn't turn me on." The rituals were never meant for the mind in the first place. Effective religious ritual touches the person in his affective depths beyond words and ideas. Loss of ritual exacts another human price. It dooms me to live at the level of the merely rational out of touch with the depths of my complete person.

Now to sum up. Chapter One was an essay in the sociology of

knowledge. There we suggested that all human knowledge is mythological in character. Myths, in the sense of the explanatory stories we tell ourselves, make up the fabric of science and morality, no less than of religion. These myths are eyeglasses through which we view the world. And since these eyeglasses are our own constructions we can put the case more actively: science, morality and religion are in the "reality-construction business." But we also suggested that our myths are not arbitrary subjective creations. One myth is not as good as another. Our myths rest at once upon a subjective act of faith and an objective test in action and experience. Chapter One stressed the subjective constructive character of religion. The chapter just concluded looked to the objective pole, the test and function of myth in action.

In its identity-giving function vis-a-vis a Transcendent Other, religious myth gives me a cosmos or a universe. I can take my bearings. I can tell what basically matters from what does not. I have some idea of where I fit into the universal scene. The story I tell myself about the drama being played out on the world stage will color all my judgments and actions. I am not a mere spectator. Religious myths give me my part, my role. We play many roles, of course, from day to day. Religious myths, however, inform me of my basic role and identity in the light of which all the others make sense. And religious myths are no mere lifeless script. They have a saving power. I often play my life part in the world drama poorly. Religious myths diagnose how and where I fall short. They not only point out my basic flaws, e.g., ignorance, attachment, sin, but show me how to be rid of them, thereby giving me the great gift of hope in the midst of evil and despair.

Religious myths also serve a community-building function. They are not vague abstractions or models presented for my contemplation as in some kind of religious fashion show. Rather they provide ritual ways of appropriating these paradigms in my own action. I am enabled to live out ritually the ideals which I am not yet able to practice in my functional day-to-day living. Ritual action keeps these "impossible" ideals alive in my life. Conversely, ritual also keeps me down to earth. By participating in baptismal rites, puberty rites, marriage rites, funeral rites, I actively assume specific responsibilities in my community. My alternatives are cut down and goals brought into focus. My life assumes a definite course and direction, rather than floating aimlessly on a sea of infinite possibilities.

In a word, religious myth gives *meaning*. Does it also give *truth*? More needs to be said about a pragmatic method of telling true myths from false, and true religion from false. We will start in the next chapter with a look at the present status of the religion game in an increasingly secular world. As we have just seen, religion can make us five ways rich. It can give us (1) a cosmos, (2) an identity, (3) a morality, (4) a hope of salvation, and (5) a freedom. Is the one without religion one who is five ways poor? Is secular society now in process of administering the last rites to religion? Or, to adapt Maritain's metaphor, will religion keep coming back to bury its undertakers?

# THREE: RELIGIOUS MYTH AS GIVER OF TRUTH

*Piety's hard enough to take*
*Among the poor who have to practice it.*
*A rich man's piety stinks. It's insufferable.*
                    *From J. B. (scene 2), Archibald Macleish*[1]


*Just as sovereign national states have become obsolete in a world*
*that can be circled in an hour and a half by man's new vehicles,*
*so have most of our explanations of the world and our systems of*
*faith become inadequate—formulated as they were in terms of a*
*quite different picture of the world than our own and within sep-*
*arate cultural communities of which some have ceased to exist.*
                    *Rolf Edberg*, On the Shred of a Cloud[2]


*When we couch behavior in the language of religion, we legi-*
*timize it; when we couch it in the language of psychiatry, we*
*illegitimize it.*
*We say that Catholics who do not eat meat on Fridays and Jews*
*who do not eat pork at all are devoutly religious; we do not say*
*that Catholics suffer from recurrent attacks of meat phobia, or*
*that Jews are afflicted with a fixed phobia of pork.*
*In the animal kingdom, the rule is, eat or be eaten; in the human*
*kingdom, define or be defined.*
                    *Thomas Szasz*, The Second Sin[3]


A question nags at the back of my head as I list all the wonder-

38

ful things that religious myth can do. "If religion is so useful," a small persistent voice urges, "then why do so many people seem to get along perfectly well without it? Aren't you overstating the case for religious myth?" Religion in America (since we are mainly concerned with the American style of playing the religion game) does seem to play a small and quite perfunctory role in the lives of most people, if indeed it has any place at all. The wall of separation between church and state has been extended to separate church from business life, political life, school life, and even family life.

It is true that an occasional priest or preacher finds his way into the political arena, but such persons quickly discover that political compromise and religious ideals are oil and water, and pretty soon are under pressure to sharply distinguish the actions performed by virtue of office from those done as religious spokesmen. And the schools. Equally effective economic pressure is being brought to bear on religiously oriented schools to divest themselves of religion as a condition for receiving the tax monies they need to survive. In Roman Catholic schools, for example, crucifixes have been stripped from the walls and shrines buried in chapel cellars. The schools are falling over each other in a headlong rush toward secularization. Money is what they need to survive. The price of government money is the governmental wall of separation between church and state.

In a sense, money tells the whole story. Where your treasure is, there also will your heart be, said Jesus. My cancelled checks tell the tale of where my values really lie. Business and religion have long enjoyed an extensive though uneasy relationship. First of all, religion is big business. Religious activities, like those of other institutions, require a broad economic support system. The day-to-day operation demands real estate, buildings, and personnel. These do not survive without income—income derived from investments in banks and corporate enterprises whose goals and ideals often fly in the face of the religious activities that draw support from them. Once again, the conflict. Like the priest-politician who is pressured to separate religion from politics, the churches are being pressured by some of their more prophetic members to disentangle their spiritual goals from messy economic involvements. And there are many others who for less prophetic reasons are only too happy to assist in the disengagement of religion from the economic sphere. Religious personnel demand economic equality with their secular counterparts, and strike to obtain it. The upshot is that the unholy alliance of religious and secularizing prophets is forcing religion out of the economic domain of human life. It is doubtful whether the product that institutional religion has to sell can survive competition in the open marketplace without those privileged exemptions that are gradually being withdrawn. People will line up for overpriced gasoline, but they were willing to boycott overpriced beef. What are the chances for religion?

The wall of separation of church and state, extended to divorce the church from the political domain, from the educational domain, and from the economic domain, is reaching now even into the sphere of family life. The wall is not quite so high, but it is growing. Marriages performed without benefit of clergy are no longer the exception. Indeed, families without benefit of marriage, while not yet the rule, are commoner every day. And children. Once their religious training could be safely assigned to the schools (private schools, Sunday schools). But these schools are fast disappearing, and parents are not taking up the slack, nor are they inclined to. The dereligionizing of the public sphere has affected (infected?) their private beliefs. It is not just a "cop-out" for them to decide to leave the question of religion to the children ("When they come of age they can make up their own minds"). More often than not, when the children come of age, religion is simply not an issue for them. They have nothing to make up their minds *about*. If you never mentioned arithmetic to children, it is unlikely they would be equipped or concerned to decide between the decimal and the binary numeral system "when they come of age." In a word, America has made religion a purely private affair. To use the sociological jargon, what has occurred is the privatization of religion.

What we have here is a new myth about religion. In Chapter One we saw religion as myth-maker. In this capacity, religion defines me in relation to others, tells me the story of the universe, and locates my place in the sun. Religion, like science and morality, is one of the ways in which the human mind produces the myths that give meaning to life and action. But now we back up one step. What is my myth about the myth-maker? What is my myth about religion itself? What meaning and sense do I give to religion? What is religion's place in the sun? If the account given in the past few pages has any merit, contemporary America has revolutionized its myth about religion. No longer, it seems, does religion provide the overarching myth by which all other myths are judged to be true or false, good or evil, meaningful or senseless. To use the sociological term, religion does not form my "inclusive" world in contemporary America. It is not part of that unshakeable taken-for-granted reality which "everybody knows" and which no one would think of questioning. In medieval Europe, in colonial and Victorian America, and in Hindu India even till today, religion formed the inclusive world, the inclusive myth which governed all the other "included" worlds, "included" myths, for example, about education, family, business, politics. These latter worlds, in the phrase of sociologist Peter Berger, were "included" under the "sacred canopy" of the all-embracing "inclusive" religious explanation. So it is no exaggeration to say that contemporary America has effected a real revolution through the privatization of religion. In making religion a purely private affair, we have, it seems, reduced religion to the status of one of those "included" worlds. Religion is no longer the privileged myth-maker governing all other myths. Religious mythology is in competition with other mythologies that are equally or more compelling. It no longer stands in judgment over them. Religion in America has successively and successfully been separated from political, educational, economic, and even family life. The recent story of religion has been one of a series of losing battles whenever it touched upon one of the vital spheres of human life. Driven from the great passionate arenas of money, sex, and power, religion seems now to exist only in isolated preserves like some pathetic species of animal in danger of extinction.

The victory in the battle of mythologies goes to the one who can define the inclusive world. And it is a battle: "define or be defined," as psychiatrist Thomas Szasz says. The dominant inclusive myth wins the day. Once upon a time the religious myth was one up. And when the religious picture of the world is what "everybody knows" to be true, then the burden of proof falls upon the one who would deny this picture. Image-making changes more lives than truth-telling. Rather, the inclusive image *is* the truth. The religious cosmic image, it seems, has become incredible. This is another way of saying that if you ask the average American the basic truth about life and the universe, he or she is more likely to answer with an economic or scientific myth than with a religious myth. What is life all about? "It's dog eat dog out there in the marketplace." "It's a spark of light produced by the evolution of the galaxies." "It's an immortal gift produced by the creative hand of God the Father." Which would your first answer be?

Define or be defined. A distraught mother brings her daughter to a mental hospital. The admission attendants take one look at the pair, and start to admit the mother. The "sick" daughter laughs. There is a flurry of embarassment until everyone sorts out who is to be defined as sick and who as well. Gambling with the bookie is a crime. Gambling with the stockmarket is an investment. Drug yourself with marijuana, and you are a pothead. Drug yourself with ethynol and you are the life of the party. To define is to control. "Black is beautiful" revolutionized the image of a race. "I'm no crook," said Nixon at a press conference, thereby admitting that Americans had succeeded in defining him as a crook. Defining even a normal child as a "slow learner" becomes a self-fulfilling prophecy. Among human beings the battle of definitions is a battle for life. And the battle to determine inclusive mythology will define the world is a battle of universes. This is the battle which religion seems to have lost.

Various diagnoses have been suggested as to what went wrong with religious myth. "Define or be defined." This slogan stresses the subjective creative side of myth. Myth determines reality. Myth is the bearer of a humanly constructed meaning. But definitions are not completely arbitrary. There is an objective control over definitions, over mythologies. There is a sense in which reality determines myth. In other words, some myths are bearers of truth as well as bearers of meaning. On the true-false scale, all myths are not of equal value. No matter how subjectively meaningful a patently false myth may appear to be, it will not work; it will lack survival value, which I will quickly find out if I try to live by it. So it is with the compulsive gambler who lives by the myth that fortune lies just around the corner; so too with the person who, high on LSD, attempts to enact the myth of "I can fly." There are religious myths, too, that run afoul of this harsh test of reality. About these myths, we cannot avoid asking, "Are they true?" Perhaps here we have a clue as to what went wrong with religious myth. Maybe some of the old myths simply do not fit new realities.

The Roman Church, for example, has a certain myth or world view or way of seeing itself when it engages in ecumenical dialogue with other churches. The Vatican Secretariate for Promoting Christian Unity in July 1975 drew up ecumenical guidelines expressing its currently operative world view. The Roman Catholic Church, it was said, considers herself the sole depository of truth even when co-operating with other Christian churches on an equal footing. This depository of truth, the Vatican went on to say, includes a firm condemnation of divorce, abortion, euthanasia, and artificial birth control. This religious mythological world view is made up of two essential correlative ingredients. First, there is the subjectively constructed meaning-factor. It expresses a cluster of attitudes, values, and imperatives to which orthodox catholics subscribe. "Every *Weltanschauung* is a conspiracy," says sociologist Peter Berger. By their Vatican-guided communal act of faith, catholics conspire to construct a world of meaning which has very definite specifications. This is a world where moral and religious truth has a unique origin (Roman Catholic

Church as sole depository); this world view is firmly opposed to the taking of human life, outside of war at any rate (condemnation of abortion and euthanasia); and this is a world that sets firm limits on the scientific control of human evolution (doctrine on artificial birth control). But this religious myth is not lived in a vacuum. Along with the subjectively constructed meaning-factor, a second correlative ingredient is part of any myth or world view. This second ingredient we can call the reality factor or truth factor. The Roman faith community is not a world unto itself. The orthodox myth confronts painful, objectively real, external challenges and checks. We saw what the Roman myth *means*; the reality-factor provokes us to ask, "Is the myth *true*?" Is the meaning factor compatible with the reality-factor? Is the myth livable in a world that is actually there and will not be wished away? The reality-factor includes the existence of rival and growing religious communities whose truth myths are utterly incompatible with the Roman one. The Roman community must live out its myth about population control in a world suffocating and starving on unchecked population growth. The reality-factor also includes men who in their intelligent and honest pursuit of truth do not condemn all abortion and all euthanasia as immoral. This is not a pitch for a "majority rules" criterion of truth. The majority can be wrong, and the minority can at times convert the majority to its own myth about the world. The only point to be made here is that the subjective act of faith must be lived out in an objectively real world. A myth will lose its hold on the mind, will lose its truth-force, to the extent that it fails to do justice to reality. Religion, as we saw, has become privatized. It no longer supplies the dominant inclusive myths by which all others are judged. The reason for religion's fall from power may lie in its failure to do justice to the way things are. If an economic myth or a scientific myth provides a much more satisfying account of the reality factor, then it is not surprising to see these myths displace the religious from its former privileged inclusive position.

Maybe we can better understand the rise and fall of the religious world view by considering for a moment a nonreligious myth that right now is in process of being dislodged from its heretofore dominant position. I refer to the impact that the reality of the ecological crisis is having on our formerly cherished image of the earth. Note first the dialectic implied here between (objective) reality and (subjective) image. Harsh reality in the shape of world famine, the shortage of fossil fuel, and the poisoning of air and water is shaking our cherished image of the earth as the repository of an inexhaustible supply of resources for human life and well-being. This myth is strong.

We will not easily let it go. It is hard to get it through our skulls that the best things in life are no longer free. And that includes water and air. It is hard to get out of that "frontier" myth, that if the supply of vital resources is depleted in one place, we can always find it somewhere else. It is hard to imagine (imagine = to form a new image) that we come to the point where that "somewhere else" does not exist. There is no more frontier. Even that last frontier—the ocean—is rapidly being staked out. Reality is forcing a new image upon our reluctant imaginations. The earth is a finite globe suspended in space and currently carrying nearly four billion human beings.

The earth as spaceship (to adopt R. Buckminster Fuller's image) is the new myth which hard ecological reality imposes. Life on a spaceship is *toto coelo* different from life on a frontier. We have not begun to appreciate the differences because our imaginations still dwell on the frontier. In a spaceship, it is one for all and all for one. An assault on fellow crew members is an assault upon oneself. War and national boundaries which seem so necessary in a frontier world become irrational and suicidal on board a spaceship. Most important of all, the earth, like the spaceship, must function as a limited self-contained biological unit. No one has put this more vividly than the well-known landscape architect and planner Ian L. McHarg. He describes the self-contained life cycle in a space capsule, and applies the model to the world:

> Inside (the capsule) was some air, some water, algae living in the water, and a man. In the water there were some bacteria as well. The system works as follows. The man breathes some air, he consumes oxygen, and breathes out carbon dioxide. The algae breathe in carbon dioxide and breathe out oxygen, which the man breathes. So there is a closed cycle of oxygen-carbon dioxide.

> The man gets thirsty, he drinks some water. He urinates, the urine goes into the water solution in which the algae live. The algae transpire, the transpirations are collected; the man drinks the condensation. So there is a closed cycle of water. The man gets hungry, he eats some algae; he defecates. The excrement goes into the water solution in which the bacteria and algae live. The bacteria break down the excrement into nutrients which are consumed by the algae, which grow, which the man eats. In this experiment, then, there is only one input, which is sunlight; there is only one output, which is heat. There is a closed cycle of oxygen and carbon dioxide, of water, of food. And the question is, "Is that the way the world works?"

And the answer is, "YOU'RE DAMN RIGHT THAT'S THE

WAY THE WORLD WORKS." . . . Anybody who doesn't know this is the way the world works—no matter what he knows —knows nothing![4]

A day of reckoning for all of us is signalled by the factory which spills tons of waste into our waters, by the tanker befouling the ocean with oil, or the city full of cars poisoning the air with carbon monoxide. There is not plenty more air where that came from. That is the frontier myth which must die before it kills us. There is not plenty more water either. We will not escape that day of reckoning any more than would a bunch of untoilet-trained astronauts confined to a small ship.

We are forced to recognize first the awesome power of myth, and secondly the crucial necessity of having the right myth. Myth's awesome power attests to its subjective creative meaning-giving function: *myth determines reality*. The need to have the right myth bears witness to the objective pole: *reality determines myth*.

Industry has flourished in America under the aegis of the all-powerful frontier myth of endlessly expanding resources and consumption. Semanticist Alfred Korzybski has said, "Those who rule our symbols rule us." Advertisers, government spokesmen, television and movie producers, and the industrial sponsors who pay them rule our symbols. And so the myth surrounding Marlboro cigarettes is not the closed cancer ward, but the open prairie (the frontier!). The myth of Schlitz beer is not a bloated stomach awash in a sea of alcoholic fumes, but a life lived with gusto on the open sea. The myth of the American auto is not that of a person trapped inside a steel box in an ocean of rush-hour fumes, but rather that of a free spirit zipping along a mountain road in solitary splendor. Thus our myth-makers artfully control us. Oscar Wilde said it more truly than perhaps he knew, "Life is an imitation of art."

Admittedly, then, myths determine reality, but not with impunity. Cancer wards and choked cities give the lie to the frontier myths that keep me smoking cigarettes and worshipping the automobile. The wrong myth makes me act against my own best interests. With the wrong myth I am like the 435 pound fat lady whose body was black and blue with bumps and bruises. She had a persistent self-image of a body half her actual size, and kept going through spaces and sitting in chairs where she could not possibly fit. Reality determines myth. If we live long enough, reality may even change our image of the earth from frontier to spaceship.

Back now to the original question. What has happened to the

powerful sway once exercised by religious mythology? That great student of myth, Joseph Campbell, has suggested that the mythologies of all the world religions fail to meet the reality test.[5] Like the ecological myth of the frontier, present religious mythologies have become outmoded, even destructive. It is not surprising that such a fate has overtaken the world religions. These faiths were formulated in cultural communities quite different from our own. Many of these communities no longer exist, and certainly their images of the world are no longer part of our thinking. Moses's band of wandering nomads, led by Yahweh their tribal God, is a universe apart from the world of modern Americans worshipping at the shrine of industry and science. But these same modern Americans go to church and synagogue only to hear stories about the tribal God. Of course, they can't believe a word of it. All the assumptions frozen into the ancient mythology clash with those of 1976's everyday world. The result is a kind of temporary suspension of belief in the world of everyday when one enters a church. It is like going to the movies. For a little while, I am lifted out of my normal attitudes, forget my troubles and play at being someone and somewhere else. The preacher adopts a different tone of voice from the one used on the golf course, and wears different clothes as well. The congregation enters into the conspiracy with songs and gestures and solemn expressions that they never use at home in the living room. But out on the sidewalk after the movie, or on the churchsteps when the communion service is over, the inclusive world of everyday takes over again. And the mythology as enacted on screen or the creed recited in church fades into unconsciousness. Their light and sound are no match for the sunlight glare outside, the roar of traffic, and the ringing of the supermarket cash register.

No wonder. Back to Moses and the Jewish religious myth, for example, of one true God and one holy race the chosen of that God. How does one get to belong to this mythologically created nation? By having a Jewish mother. This is the traditional answer and the official policy of the Jewish state today. Out of all the races on earth, God has made a special covenant or agreement with this one race. This myth strikes profound emotional chords in the Jewish heart, but at the price of intellectual dissonance. For though Yahweh is addressed as Lord of the Universe, he is essentially a tribal god who has no *special* concern, say, for Asia's teeming millions or for the Indio-Christians of Latin America.

In the Christian myth as well, God is no less tied up with a limited historical social institution. Baptism is the initiation rite. This links the Christian to Jesus Christ who was true man. And because

Jesus was miraculously true God as well, this links the Christian to God. The membership requirement is not biological as in the Jewish myth, but juridical, and thus theoretically open to every human being. It is unimaginable that the billions of Buddhists, Hindus and Marxists should even consider membership in such an alien institution as a condition for *their* particular brands of salvation. In fact, for the Hindu it is no miracle at all that Jesus Christ is true God and true man. Everybody is. It is up to each person to wake up to this fact. It is ludicrous to the Hindu that divine life should be channelled through a conditioned historical social institution. Again, the myth of union with Christ evokes deep emotional reverberations in the Christian. But Christianity's imperialist claim that the whole human race is destined to belong to this particular institution becomes more and more incredible in a global perspective where Christians form an ever-shrinking minority.

These observations are not intended to trivialize the myths of the great world religions. In fact, the last chapter was a litany of the vital human functions performed by these myths even today. We merely wish to point out that in spite of this vitality these religions are sick. This book is a search for a provisional diagnosis and a suggestion toward a cure. If a mythology is to stay alive and strong, the image of the universe that it offers should be consistent with the totality of knowledge of its own day. When the religious myth clashes too violently with contemporary scientific, moral, and other myths, something has got to give. Not surprisingly, the religious myths of the great oriental and occidental religions are 2000 years out of date: they presuppose the cosmology and imagery that flourished in the communities where these mythologies were born. Thus we have the early Vedic hymns of Hinduism supposing an environment in which a multitude of gods directed the play of natural forces—fire, sunlight, flood, drought, rain and the growth of crops. We have, originating in Mesopotamia and adopted by Christianity, those religious mythologies modelled on the hierarchical order of celestial mathematics in which the heavenly spheres follow their predictable paths "the lowest subject to the midmost, and the midmost subject to the uppermost" as St. Ignatius Loyola says in his letter on obedience. In this geography, the privileged cosmic place is the heavens, and life on earth looks there for its guidance. It was Bethlehem's star in the night skies that announced to the priestly watchers the Messiah's coming. And the Messiah's going? Also to the heavens in the myth of Christ's ascension to this privileged cosmic place which is the focal point of earthly life. And in the myth, it *is* a place. The ascension is a *bodily* one, as is Mary's assumption into heaven and Elijah's ascent. But Galileo showed that there is nothing special about the heavens. Celestial bodies follow the same laws as do earthly. The moon is "out there" from the vantage point of earth, and earth is "out there" from the vantage point of the moon. So where is God? Where are those assumed and resurrected bodies? Where is the focal point of human life?

Christian theologians will rightly point out that such questions are neither original nor new. They pointed this out to Bishop John A. T. Robinson when he railed against a God "out there" in the first days of the "God is Dead" movement, now itself dead. To be sure, these myths were taken literally in the settings in which they were born. The ancient cosmologies supported the ancient images. As cosmologies changed through the centuries, an increasing strain was put on the spiritual truths that these ancient images were meant to express. Theologians have not been remiss in their efforts to "demythologize," as they call it, religious teaching. But to demythologize is a risky business. If all knowledge is mythological, as the first chapter claims, then to demythologize a teaching is to destroy it. Theologians have tried manfully to disengage the allegedly abiding spiritual "truth" from the transitory and conditioned "myths" in which the truths were embodied. The heavens were no longer to be the physical geographical place envisaged by Jesus, Aquinas, and Dante. Such physical images are to be interpreted mystically, spiritually, symbolically. A contemporary spiritual truth is enshrined in an ancient spiritual image. Thus the schizophrenia experienced in church between clashing world views becomes less acute—at least for the theological sophisticate. There is still a dualism, but no longer is it a clash between a literal ancient cosmology and a literal modern one. The ancient cosmology has been spiritualized. It is not to be understood literally. On these revised terms, it can more easily coexist with the contemporary literal cosmos. And incidentally, the focal point of human life can be moved back down from the mythological heavens to the *terra firmior* of the earth and human experience. To replace the heavens with the earth in the new cosmology is not to lay claim to a new-found truth. The new cosmology is as mythological as the old but it is a myth that we can more easily live with.

The more orthodox theologians, at any rate, have not merely demythologized religion, but have remythologized it. This is a crucial distinction. As we noted above, to demythologize alone is to destroy, since knowledge if it is not mythological is nothing. If you take away the myths from human knowledge with the goal of accepting only the residue, you are in danger of discovering that there is no residue. Thus when Bultmann demythologized the New Testament regarding the historicity of Christ, he could conclude to only one residual truth, viz., there was a man named Christ and he died. To reach this conclusion, he applied to the gospels the textual critical norms of modern historiography. I suggest he did not go far enough. What he has done is to give historiographical myth precedence over religious myth. He should have demythologized the historical myth as well. Then the destruction would have been complete.[6]

More interesting is the sophisticated attempt of orthodox theologians to remythologize. This book, though philosophical rather than theological in character, is an effort in that direction. As we saw above, one common ploy of current Christian remythologizers is to turn physical truths into spiritual ones. A case could be made that the remythologizing process, as carried out in Christianity at any rate, has succeeded all too well. For all its creaky apparatus of outdated imagery, religious mythology packs a tremendous wallop. In spite of the conscious dissonance that religious mythology can generate, it has its greatest impact on the unconscious springs of action as we saw in the last chapter. We have been speaking of theological efforts to remythologize religion in order to ameliorate the conscious dissonance between old and modern cosmologies. University of California historian Lynn White has suggested that Christianity needs to be remythologized so as to redirect its impact on our unconscious.[7] Conscious "doublethink" is not the only thing wrong with religious mythology. More profoundly than anything conscious, Christian mythology shapes our unconscious assumptions about the modern world in positively destructive ways, says White. We need to make conscious these unconscious religious assumptions and give them more appropriate form. White's basic indictment is that the Christian myth about our relation to nature legitimates and solidifies the present destructive environmental attitudes that are heading us toward race suicide.

How we treat our environment, says White, is conditioned deeply by our religious beliefs concerning human nature and destiny. Christian thinking is permeated by three myths that are foreign to Oriental religious mythology. These three myths, in White's view, have fostered not only the rise of science and technology, but also an exploitive attitude toward nature. The ruthless character of technological rationality is sustained by the Hebraeo-Christian myths (1) of progress, (2) of a dualism of man and nature, and (3) of nature as the embodiment of God's purposes.

We may live in the "post-Christian era" in terms of church affiliation, but our feelings and actions are saturated with the peculiarly Christian view of history, humanity and nature. Fundamental is the myth of progress. Time is not an endlessly recurring cycle of events, as the Hindu viewed it. The world does not extend infinitely and endlessly into the past, as in the Graeco-Roman accounts. No, history has a beginning, a middle, and an end: it is the inexorable working out of a divine plan. History is salvation history, and human beings are at the center.

Further, humans, though made of clay, are not merely part of nature. Nature and everything in it is destined for people, and people for God. We share God's transcendence of nature. We are to exploit nature's resources, dominate it for our own ends. In this way, we fulfill the divine plan. Built into the Christian myth is this dualism of *humanity* transcending *nature* which is divinely destined to be subordinate.

And since nature is the product of God's creative hand, the struggle to understand how nature operates was seen as the struggle to understand God's mind. In wresting from nature its secrets, one learned the natural law which is the reflection of the eternal law. The scientific work of Roger Bacon, Leibniz, Galileo, and Newton was explicitly compelled by this religious motivation. What we view as scientific insights, to these men were theological as well—even primarily theological. In this cultural climate, where one saw oneself as the divinely appointed dominator of nature, science and technology grew up and flourished. Nowhere more clearly than in Teilhard de Chardin do we have expressed this anthropocentric dualism of humanity's gradually evolving conquest of nature through which we, finally leaving nature behind, will arrive at the ultimate goal of divinization through union with the transcendent Christ.

The religious legitimation of this way of thinking has receded somewhat from the Western secular consciousness, but our transcendence over nature, and adversary relation to it, is an unquestioned part of our taken-for-granted world. In this spirit, we undertake incessant *wars* against poverty, against crime, against overpopulation, against fuel shortage, against food shortage, against illiteracy—no problem too great that we cannot overcome it, add to our conquests. To the Westerner, this is an obvious realistic healthy attitude, at least until we take a serious look at other religious myths that undermine our own. The destructiveness of the traditional Christian myth, according to White, lies precisely in this dualism: we locate ourselves *apart* from nature, instead of seeing ourselves as *part* of nature, and hence part of those problems we project onto nature. Such a myth can no longer sustain our attempts to survive in the world we know today. There is a religious mythic vacuum that needs to be filled. This chapter's probings into the deficiencies of religious myth as bearer of truth is not a call for the end of religion, but for religion remythologized. A new world calls for a new myth.

That bluish green ball suspended in space and photographed for us by the astronauts—this is our shattering new image of the world. Hear Joseph Campbell:

> Our astronauts on the moon have pulled the moon to earth and sent the earth soaring to heaven. From the deserts of Mars this Mother Earth of ours will be again seen, higher, remoter, more heavenly still; yet no nearer to any god than right now.[8]

This is not merely a matter of intellect. We can no longer *feel* the same about either the world or our gods. To such an image of the world, our political maps with their angry lines dividing nation from nation become absurdly inadequate. The surface of this earth is an island floating on one world ocean and bathed by the continuously swirling winds and clouds. The gods of this new world cannot be imagined to dwell in the heavens. Indeed this world is in the heavens. The divine spirit, if it is to be found anywhere, is to be found on earth. Rival gods and rival religions are equally as absurd as rival nation states in this new image of the world. A remythologized religion, if it is to do its job, must hit us where it counts, in our affect system; it must be responsive to our new feeling about the world. For this new feeling about the world guarantees that we can never feel the same again about ourselves as human beings, or about our God. The old mythologies fail precisely insofar as they trap us into old and inappropriate ways of feeling, and therefore of acting. We will start to outline in part the shape that a new and more appropriate mythology might take. We will look into the resources of American pragmatism for the tools to accomplish the task.

In conclusion, we have seen that in America religion has lost the privileged place it once had. Religion has become a private affair, divorced from mainstream living. The worlds of business, politics, education, and even family life go their own independent ways. No longer does religious mythology supply the inclusive world by which these other worlds are judged. Why has religious myth lost its grip on our lives? We suggested a two-fold diagnosis.

First, the mythologies of the great world religions conflict with the contemporary pictures we have of the world. They have become outmoded. In ecology, earth as spaceship is replacing the destructive image of earth as frontier. The latter myth no longer does the job. So, too, religious mythology no longer does the job of making sense of the world we know today. Only at the cost of a "doublethink" mentality can religious mythology coexist with present day myths. Secondly, we suggested that at least the Christian myth has in some ways become destructive. In its excessive humanism, it has become antihuman. Religious mythology is perhaps not merely irrelevant, but harmful.

We do not, however, prescribe the end of religion. Religion, as we saw in the last chapter, can perform great services for mankind. Religions need to be demythologized of their inappropriate and harmful images. But the prescription does not end there. They need to be remythologized so that they can resume the beneficial functions they once performed so well. This is a large order and is beyond the scope of this book. We intend in the following chapters only to suggest some tools and directions for the task at hand of remythologizing religion.

# PART TWO
# THE AMERICAN STYLE

# FOUR: FAITH: THE RELIGIOUS WORLD IS YOURS TO BUILD

*It is only by risking our persons from one hour to another that we live at all. And often enough our faith beforehand in an uncertified result is the only thing that makes the result come true.*[1]

*If we survey the field of history and ask what feature all great periods of revival, of expansion of the human mind, display in common, we shall find, I think, simply this: "The inmost nature of reality is congenial to the powers which you possess."*[2]

William James

Needless to say, the first part of this book does not begin to tell the full story about the religion game. We did see some of the good and bad things religion can do, and we did note some of the ways religion stacks up against other games we play and other myths we live by. Neither will Part Two tell the full story about the American style of playing the religion game. We will draw chiefly upon that quintessentially American philosophy of the past one hundred years —pragmatism; we will note some of the ways that this particularly American philosophical myth can enlighten both our understanding and our living of religion. Lurking in the background will be those giants of American philosophy, William James, Charles S. Pierce, John Dewey, George Herbert Mead, as well as the contemporary thinkers who have applied to religion the insights elaborated by these great men. What follows is neither a history of pragmatism nor an attempt to expound the religious philosophies of the pragmatists. We will make some suggestions for a philosophy of religion based upon

55

what John J. McDermott has called "The American Angle of Vision." Experience, freedom, and action will be keynote themes. I invite you to get into the pragmatic way of thinking for a little while. I hope that this will bring some new depth of insight into the religious dimension of experience.

At first glance, religion and pragmatism might seem to be strange bedfellows indeed. Pragmatism has connotations of expediency, materialism, naturalism, and devotion to the almighty dollar. In fact, one of pragmatism's founders, William James, to his undying regret once spoke of the pragmatic emphasis on the "cash value" of ideas, an image which his critics seized upon as proof that this philosophy was no more than a nasty materialism. We will not argue the point here. Rather, in a pragmatic vein, we invite you to take a look and see what this philosophy has to offer for religion, and then judge for yourself.

Pragmatism has a fresh way of looking at religion. In my view, it is just what the doctor ordered, especially for Americans. Pragmatism is neither an outmoded myth nor a foreign import. It makes explicit for us many of the day-to-day assumptions that form our inclusive taken-for-granted world. So when we look at religion through pragmatic eyeglasses, it comes into focus and assumes its rightful place in our lives. For it is through these same eyeglasses that we view the other dimensions of our lives as well. No more need for "doublethink." Wear the same eyeglasses in church and outside. Pragmatism helps you be just as intelligent, experimental and free about religion as you are about any other area of your life. Religion need not be a peculiar or abrasive world if you can express and live it through a myth with which you are thoroughly at home. For Americans, pragmatism is just such a myth. The next few chapters will tell the pragmatic story about religion. We start here with *faith*. William James will be our storyteller, and his famous essay, "The Will to Believe," our principal guide.

Many of us, says James, have nagging in the back of our heads the little boy's definition of faith as "believing something that you know ain't true."[3] Faith, it seems, is opposed to reason. Hard-nosed intelligence demands evidence: seeing is believing. Soft-headed faith believes where there is no evidence: "Blessed are they who have not seen but have believed." Are we to say that the believer has no intellectual self-respect? Is the attitude of faith stupid and irrational? Is the believer thereby acting in a less than human way? No! says William James, "The believer is the true full man." It is rather the doubting Thomas and the man from Missouri who are destined to live lives that are less than human. Faith opens up human possibilities, hypotheses for action, that are sealed off from the person who insists on proof.

Note the pragmatic stress on *action*. Faith is so crucially important because of its impact on action. An act of faith is a decision between hypotheses for action. Call such a decision an *option*. An option, to be genuine, has to grab me, has to put me to the test of action. An option does this when it has three qualities. A genuine option must be (1) living, (2) forced, and (3) momentous.

A live option is one that makes a genuine appeal to me; I would be willing to act upon it. Shall I pay a call on Jacqueline Onassis or on Julie Eisenhower? For me, this is not a living option. It is incredible that I should call on either of these two ladies. But such an option may well be a living one for the editor of *Cosmopolitan* magazine. Similarly, the decision whether to become a Shintoist or a snakeworshipper is a dead option as far as I am concerned, but the option to believe in nihilism rather than in immortality is very much alive: it is credible to me that I could act on either hypothesis.

A genuine option is not only living, but it is *forced*. "Choose," I ask you, "between the brown hat and the blue one." Such a choice is easily avoidable: "I don't wear hats," you answer. But if I ask an alcoholic, "Are you going to face up to the fact that you are drinking yourself to death, or are you going to go on pretending?" that person has no out. The option is unavoidable—forced.

Finally, a genuine option is *momentous*, not trivial. "Shall I give the paper boy four nickles or two dimes?"—no genuine option here. The decision is too trivial to involve my attention. More momentous would be a decision to seize a new job offered to me in Tokyo, rather than sticking with my familiar one in Peoria. This would be a genuine option.

To believe or not to believe: (1) that Christ rose from the dead and is alive today, (2) that there is no God and that this life is all there is, (3) that all things are God: *Atman* is *Brahman*. Could you care less about any of these beliefs? Faith, for the pragmatist, is no empty formalism. Only genuine options—live, forced momentous—count. Beliefs are for the sake of life. No matter how religiously you recite them in the creed, beliefs are only pseudo-beliefs unless they somehow hook into your living *action*-al life. A *trivial* option does not do this. If the option as to whether or not to go to church on Sunday is trivial to you, then this no more belongs in your religious ballpark than it would in that of a devout Marxist. And an *avoidable* option does not necessarily hook into my pragmatic life. If, for example, a Jewish couple can and rather easily does avoid the option whether or not to be married before a rabbi by the simple expedient of living together without benefit of synagogue, then this is not part of their ongoing faith game. It is not even something for them to reject. They avoid the issue altogether. And a *dead* option has nothing to do with genuine faith. If eager devotees of the Krishna Consciousness Society accost a little old lady on her way to daily Mass, in no way could they confront her with a living appeal to action. Life as a devotee of Krishna is just not in her realm of possibilities. It is incredible that she could even consider donning a saffron robe, shaving her head and chanting Krishna's praises to the beat of bongo drums. No need for her to reject the possibility. The issue just could not come up; the option is dead.

So, for the pragmatist, faith does not belong to the realm of abstraction. It is not something apart from everyday life, not a list of propositions to be proved or disproved, accepted or rejected, whether or not I care about them. If someone raises a question to you about religion, or God, or immortality, or the soul, and it just makes you want to yawn, then forget it. It is just not part of your faith game. It is not a genuine option. It is not worth wasting your time over, no matter how much it sounds like something you *should* believe in, you *should* care about, or that *should* affect your life and action. If it doesn't, it doesn't. Until it does make such an appeal to you, it is only masquerading as genuinely possible belief. Faith is genuine only when it can make a difference in living.

So we are dealing with dynamite. "Handle with care!" The life you change may be your own. How cautious should we be? In matters of faith, does supercaution pay off? Note well the words "pay off"— the pragmatist thinks in terms of consequences. You can assume two opposing attitudes vis-a-vis religious faith (or indeed toward any kind of faith): (1) that of stubborn hard-nosed empiricism that demands proof every step of the way; (2) that of the "will to believe" that surrenders to faith and lets it work on you. What is the payoff, what are the consequences of each of these two attitudes?

It depends, says James, on what kind of hypothesis you are talking about. The scientific truth game, generally, plays by rules that are different from the religion game. To apply to the latter the rules of the former just does not pay off. Pay off in what coin? The coin of reaching and living the truth. Over the doorway leading into the scientific lab a warning is posted: "Avoid error; demand proof; verify your hypotheses." This motto has paid off in space labs, moon walks, and astronaut landings predicted to the very minute. This is not to deny, as we saw in Chapter One, that scientific research has its subjective side. The space program rested, for example, on acts of faith that the scientific method would continue to work, that the moon landing was worth the effort, that the national will and support for the project would persist over the long haul, and that the laws of gravity would not be arbitrarily suspended. Bur granting that the scientific myth resembles the religious in this subjective pole, James sees a crucial distinction between science and religion on the objective side. Both scientific faith and religious faith must meet the objective test of reality. But this objective test operates differently in religion from the way it does in science. The aim of science is to reach true scientific beliefs, i.e., beliefs whose consequences for action will enrich and expand my understanding of the world. One of the aims of religion is to reach true religious beliefs whose consequences for action will expand and integrate my life. The scientific payoff is best assured by careful empirical verification of every hypothesis. Avoid error. Accept nothing that cannot be objectively verified by publicly repeatable experiments. But you will fail miserably, says James, if you try to apply this same sort of objective test to religion. The payoff will not be there. Worse, you would thereby close off the very possibility of experiencing in your life the benefits of true religious beliefs.

This is not to deny the objective pole of religious myths. No less than science, religious faith must meet the challenge of objective testing in reality. But to make religion walk the *scientific* path of objective testing is to misconstrue the religion game completely. Blackjack is not poker. Anyone who keeps insisting in a game of blackjack that the dealer pay off for a Full House is a guaranteed loser. Anyone who insists on submitting religious beliefs to laboratory tests has no idea what the religion game is all about. Such a person is a guaranteed loser—worse, not even a player, missing the point completely when demanding an observable repeatable objective test for such religious hypotheses as "God exists," "There is a loving Providence," "Christ rose from the dead," "There is a life after death." There is an objective side to religious myth, but it is not to be found through observable scientific experimentation.

Science and religion are each concerned with different types of hypotheses for action. This accounts for the different kinds of truth game that each involves. The decision as to whether or not to accept a scientific hypothesis as true is not a *genuine* option. The scientist can afford to wait for results. Seldom is the hypothesis at stake so momentous that he or she can risk being duped by prematurely accepting its truth. Occasionally, a scientist so falls in love with the hypothesis that he or she sees evidence which is not there or even doctors the evidence. Such a one the scientific establishment will quickly and roundly condemn.

Occasionally, however, the hypothesis *is* momentous. Consider the case of a young child dying of cancer when all known remedies have been exhausted. A new and as yet untested drug appears on the scene. The option as to whether or not to administer the drug—to treat it as a true cure—is now a genuine option. (I am going to delay a moment on this, because I think it parallels the case of religion's genuine options.) At stake is life or death: the option is *momentous*, not trivial. And it is a *forced* option. Either I administer the drug or I do not; there is no running away from the issue. And, finally, it is a *live* option. It makes a vivid appeal to action. Doctor, family, and patient agonize over the pro's and con's.

Let us see now how the truth game changes, even in the case of science, when the option involved is a *genuine* one. First, what would be the ordinary rules about an untested hypothesis concerning a new cancer cure? Obviously, the new drug would be tested. Its use for human beings would not even be considered until the observable experimental results were in. These results would be verified repeatedly under controlled conditions and in different circumstances to eliminate extraneous variables. Only after the drug had met these stringent empirical tests could truth claims about its efficacy be legitimately made. Such would be the ordinary rules for the scientist in the research laboratory. It is not a *genuine* option whether or not to accept the truth of the hypothesis. It is not momentous; there is no hurry to use the drug. The scientist would rather wait and be sure than leap prematurely and be wrong. The option is not forced. In the detached laboratory atmosphere there is no pressure to decide whether or not to administer it. So neither is it a live option whether to use an untested drug. It makes no appeal to this action. In fact, it would not even be considered. So much for the ordinary rules.

Now back to the bedside of the dying young cancer patient. The option that was trivial, avoidable, and dead in the lab, becomes momentous, forced and live in the hospital. The rules of the truth game that pay off in the lab will not necessarily pay off in the hospital. In the lab, the motto is to avoid error, to demand rigorous proof before acting. In the hospital no such atmosphere of leisurely detachment prevails. There, the option is genuine. The decision involves life and death; it must be made now, before all the results are in; and the participants are keenly aware both of the need to decide and of the possible consequences of their decision. Would you insist that they apply laboratory rules? Would you forbid them to consider administering the untested drug? Both in the lab and in the hospital, the aim—the payoff—is a true belief, a belief that will enrich action and life, here, a belief in a cancer cure. What is that dying patient's best path to the truth of this belief? Does the risk of premature belief outweigh the risk of being wrong? To this question the research scientist answered yes. But what about the patient?

The logic is clear. The drug may well be a true cure. But the patient will never benefit from that truth if the researcher's cautious skepticism is followed. The patient's best and only course is to stake his life on the truth of this hypothesis. Otherwise, this child stands to lose all. Faith in the cure—even in a cure as yet unproved—is the best path to take. But the patient may be deceived, you say; the drug might not be a true cure at all. So the hope is deceiving him. Is that any worse than being duped by fear of error if indeed the cure would have worked? It is even possible that hope could create its own verification; belief in the drug could help the drug to work. You are more likely to lose the truth than gain it, says James, if you play by scientific rules when a genuine option is at stake. And this is especially the case with religion.

If you are indifferent to religion, James is not talking to you. Neither is he if you have merely a detached scientific interest in religion. But if religious belief is a genuine option for you, then no one has the right—even on logical grounds—to caution you to suspend your belief while waiting for proof. Recall from Chapter Two all the things that religion can do for you. Must fear of error cause you to risk losing all this meaning? Of course not, says James. And such faith is not anti-intellectual, any more than was the dying patient's faith in the curative drug. Faith was the most reasonable response of a person in the face of a genuine religious option. One feels the call of a divine dimension of living beyond the world of everyday. Religion, then, is a living option, and momentous, too; one's whole life will be different depending on the response. And the option is forced; "yes" or "no," there is no avoiding the issue. How could it be reasonable to close off the possibility of this whole dimension of life in the name of awaiting an empirical proof that is never to be forthcoming? As James bluntly puts it:

> a rule of thinking which would absolutely prevent me from acknowledging certain kinds of truth if those kinds of truth were really there, would be an irrational rule.[4]

And the response of faith is all the more reasonable if this divine dimension is *personal*. Faith and trust lie at the heart of interpersonal relations. The man who demands proof that a marriage will work before he proposes marriage will never walk down the aisle. His attitude effectively closes him off from the whole dimension of married living. His very demand for proof of its true worth ensures that he will never know its true worth. Conversely, faith and trust in another's worth can make that fact come true; whence we have the phenomenon of the self-fulfilling prophecy. As James points out: "How many women's hearts are vanquished by the mere sanguine insistence of some man that they *must* love him! He will not consent to the hypothesis that they cannot."[5] Similarly our relations with a personal God are best governed by willing faith rather than by scientific detachment. The mind is not the only pathway to truth. Where genuine options are at stake, it is the will that opens us up to truth. James places himself squarely in the tradition of Augustine: *credo ut intelligam*: "I believe that I may understand."

However, I cannot with impunity conjure up beliefs out of thin air. Upon my faith rests the meaning of my life, but I cannot create meaning arbitrarily and irresponsibly. Faith is a way of life, a recipe for living, a method. It opens me up to dimensions of living that without faith would remain closed. And right here we have the test that my faith must meet. Does it really open up for me new dimensions of experience, new facets of living? The meaning of my life is not the product of faith alone. Meaning is generated by the interaction of my faith with the world in which I live. A genuine faith is one that fosters this interaction. Whatever be the origin of my faith— Sunday school, books, psychological crisis, or instruction at my mother's knee—that faith must meet the pragmatic test. James and the pragmatist are concerned with the consequences of faith, rather than with its origins. Genuine faith serves life, opens up unsuspected possibilities, unleashes my latent energies. Genuine faith points to a world that is friendly to me, that says "yes" to the powers I have and to the person I would like to become. In the words of James, a life-serving faith attests that "the inmost nature of reality is congenial to the powers which you possess."[6] Different men have different powers and so it is not surprising that different faiths inspire them. But every faith that has caught on with humankind has been distinguished by this one trait: it shows the universe to be friendly and supportive of the things we want to do and be.

A faith that kills—that faith itself deserves to die. Every genuine faith gives life. Christianity, for example, broke loose upon the pagan world precisely because it brought life to the weak, the downtrodden, the sinners. Whatever bad I have done and however weak I am, Christianity told me that at least I can repent. This power to repent, which the weakest person has, Christianity made into a "hot line" leading directly to the heart of God. In similar fashion, Reformation faith burst in upon the medieval papist world. Self-despair and faith are powers that any man can summon. The reformers unleashed these powers by showing that they could be exercised by the individual face to face with God, bypassing all oppressive priestly mediation. Such are James's examples of life-giving faith. You might ask yourself what is the appeal of insurgent religious movements in America today —Pentecostalism, the Jesus Movement, ISKCON, and what has been dubbed "The New Counter-Reformation." What pent-up powers do these faiths release? Answer this question, and you will see in what way each is a faith in the service of life. Each is a faith which enables its believers to interact with the world in new and hitherto unsuspected ways. By hooking the believer into this new world with its creative possibilities, faith serves as midwife to fresh "meanings of life." Faith, for the pragmatist, is not irrational and stifling. The pragmatic test demands that faith give life if it is to merit its name. Far from being irrational, faith in its life-giving function is the very source of meaning and rationality.

So faith in general, and religious faith in particular, is not a matter of "anything goes." The pragmatic test of faith is that it nourish life and rationality. "Woe to him," says James, "whose beliefs play fast and loose with the order which realities follow in his experience; they will lead him nowhere or else make false connexions."[7] But though faith must undergo the objective testing of lived experience, this does not mean that any one faith or set of beliefs is best for all. Pragmatism is perfectly at home in a pluralistic religious world. The faith that nurtures you might suffocate me. This is not to say that your belief world is either better or worse than mine. It is different, that's all; and you and I are different. Boston is not Bombay, and Father Drinan is not Swami Satchitananda. And the Boston and Bombay of a hundred years ago are different from those places today, and from what they will be a hundred years hence. The pragmatist's religious faith is responsive to the process and pluralism of the world in which one lives.

So the American style of playing the religion game supposes a characteristically American philosophy about the world in which that game is played. That world, first of all, is open-ended and unfinished; it is still in process; *novelty* results from my interaction with such a world of creative possibilities. Variety is the second keynote of

James's view of the world; there are many levels and kinds of entities, many different perspectives and ways of being; the world is not reducible to any one stuff, be it "Spirit," "Matter," "Life," or "Consciousness;" the world is *pluralistic*. Thirdly, these entities, for all their rich and endless variety, are connected; there are continuities, there is *relatedness* between myself and the world in which I act; my field of action finds relatives and friends as well as strangers. "Radical Empiricism" is the fancy philosophical label that James gives to this world of novelty, pluralism, and relatedness. Let us see what religious faith looks like in a novel, pluralistic and continuous world.

First, in a Jamesian world, novelty is a sign of faith. No place here for a Holy Office (Roman Christianity's watchdog over faith, where novelty is viewed as the very essence of heresy). What is suspect now is not a faith that changes, but a faith that adheres unswervingly to dogmas that never change. "I believe in novelty" is the first article of this pragmatic creed. The unexpected is expected. A living faith must evolve and change. Herein lies survival.

Well, is "pop theology" to be the norm? Should we now speak of fads rather than of faith? Is the true believer now reduced to asking the incessantly superficial question "What's new?" Pop theology fails precisely insofar as it absolutizes the present. Today's novelty is tomorrow's platitude. Nothing is so downright embarrassing as yesterday's fad today. Whatever became of hula-hoops? They went the same path of that God who was alleged to be dead.

Pragmatism's faith in novelty is not an idolatry of the present. Rather, it is rooted in the past and points toward the future. It is not locked in the ever-vanishing present. Scientific method and evolutionary theory are the parents of pragmatism's religious world. A pragmatist's faith is conservative. Novelty is in the service of survival. As in biological evolution, it is the fittest faith that survives. As with scientific method, novelty is cherished to the extent that it adapts new data to the corpus of what is already known. As John Dewey remarked, outmoded hypotheses do not need to be refuted; they die a natural death. The same goes for outmoded faith. A faith that is unable to adapt to novelty will wither and die.

So pragmatic faith is not concerned with the ever-changing fads that answer the question "What's new?" Much more profoundly it is concerned with the question of "What is best?" or "What is fittest?" It is novelty in the service of the best, in the service of the fittest, and therefore in the service of survival. Those survive best who can accommodate the novel and unexpected. Put another way, a living act of faith is a creative act.

Recall our working definition of the religion game. It embraces all those human activities and attitudes which have ultimate reality as their goal, and the achievement of full human potential as their motivation. What James points out is simply this: in a world characterized by novelty, this game must be played creatively, if it is to be played at all. In my search for the ultimate meaning of my life, I can never relax and say I have finally figured it out; I have finished; I know what it is all about. There are moments of rest, certitude and religious ecstasy, to be sure. But the world turns, evolution courses on, and novelty crashes in to break the spell. And my faith is tested. Am I strong enough to respond to this novelty and create the new religious meaning my heart desires and demands?

The exigencies of worldwide hunger and of the burgeoning world population, for example, are "novelties" which challenge the creativity of religious myths in both the East and the West. Consider the following creative adaptation of a traditional humanistic myth. Some advocates of the humanistic moral myth are urging on the developed nations a "Lifeboat Ethics" regarding the rest of mankind. The traditional myth had expressed unconditional concern for every human being. In the new myth, that concern is conditional. Aid to underdeveloped countries, it is contended, should be predicated upon their willingness to undertake effective population control. Lifeboat Earth cannot support everybody. If nations will not control their populations, let them sink. This is one creative adaptation of humanism to the novel reality of massive overpopulation and famine.

Some players of the Hindu religion game are speaking in new accents of industrialization and material development. The traditional game rules had stipulated detachment from the world of sense and banishment of the illusion of individuality. How is this old game to be played in the harsh "novel" world of famine and overpopulation? To survive it has to creatively adapt. Material detachment and enlightenment are still goals in the reconstructed myth of modern Hinduism. But there is a new emphasis on the *stages* of spiritual progress. The possibility of enlightenment presupposes first a sufficiency of health and material things. Thus a space is made in the old game for the rules of modern industrialization. And the Hindu myth survives.

Creative response to novelty need not always involve rejection of the traditional myth. Sometimes the tradition is more right than we know. Tampering with it can provoke a novel and unexpected backlash: the new jolting us back to the old. Doctrinaire liberal Christianity recently received such a jolt at the 1974 World Population Conference held in Bucharest. Liberal Christians had accepted the scientific myth about the need for technologically limiting population growth. This technological solution was roundly rejected by the Third World bloc (which might better be called the Two-Thirds World bloc, for such is the proportion of population relative to the rest of the world). This was a rude shock to the Christian West, which had complacently diagnosed a "problem" here of overpopulation, and a solution: the life-force is producing too many people!—the solution is to technologically intervene in the life-force to limit procreation.

This "obvious" answer was not so obvious to the nations of the Third World. They preferred not to tamper with the life-force technologically, but rather to trust it. Unwittingly they were urging on Christians their own traditional natural law taboo against artificial contraception! The problem, in the view of the Third World, is not overpopulation at all. The problem is rather the unequal and unjust distribution of the world's resources. Instead of restricting the right of the poor to have children, the developed nations should cut down their own over-consumption, and cut out exploitation, so that the poor nations may share more equitably in the world's resources. This done, the poor will limit their own procreation without manipulative controls imposed from the outside. The affluent nations stand as a living proof of this thesis. As human material well-being and security increase, population decreases. The United States now enjoys a zero population growth without the mandatory controls it would like to impose upon the poor nations as a condition for receiving aid. This "novel" and unexpected response challenges the Christian West to return to the traditional rules of its religion game: trust life; trust nature; treat all with justice, and nature will take care of itself!

A final observation on the need to accommodate to the "novel" dimension of experience: it need not always be the *religious* myth that has to do the accommodating. Scientific myths occupy a privileged position in today's world. Pragmatism itself was born of a desire to bring philosophical method into line with the scientific, and to accommodate philosophy to a world revolutionized by Darwin's evolutionism and Watson's behaviorism. So pragmatism accorded an ascendency to the reigning psychological and biological myths of science, and so as a matter of history scientific mythology rather than religious played the greater part in fathering pragmatic philosophy. But the privileged place of science need not be a matter of principle. The fullest humanistic experiential development of man may be just as well served by according a primacy to religious myths over scientific. It is conceivable that religious myth might best pass the pragmatic test of action that maximizes human survival and growth. The minimum demand of pragmatic faith is that religion live in a world that is characterized by novelty, where the unexpected is expected, and where attempts by religious faith to freeze experience into rigid dogmatic forms will only lead to religion's demise.

Not only novelty, but *pluralism* too, characterizes James's world of radical empiricism. The pragmatic religion game not only expects variety, but joyfully embraces it. The "good-guy" world is not *one*, but *many*; it takes all kinds—all kinds of religions, rites, worshippers, codes, creeds, ideas of God. Experience is inexhaustibly diverse. And pragmatic religious faith reflects this diversity. There is no one true faith, one true ritual, one true morality, one true conception of God, one true prophet, one true incarnation. A pluralistic world where true diversity reigns gives the lie to attempts to extract a true anything. The price of focusing on the one is to ignore the many. But the many will not go away. The many comes back to haunt those who try to believe in only one.

Reductionism is a disease endemic to the philosophical and religious mind. There is a hankering to reduce reality or faith or God to only one kind of stuff. The world is pluralistic, religionists like to say, but basically, if we only look deep enough, it is one. The founders of pragmatism grew up in a world of idealistic philosophy in which such monism (one-ism) was rampant. In reaction to this, James especially insisted upon the pluralistic character of the universe. A pluralistic religious world will resist both false ecumenism and its opposite, dogmatic confessionalism.

An ecumenism that glosses over the real differences among various religious traditions is untrue to such a pluralistic world. At the other extreme, a dogmatic confessional faith that claims to have a hold on the one true religion is equally unfaithful to the diversity that characterizes our universe. The differences are just as real as the similarities. So those efforts fail that try to make pluralism take second place to unity. Such, for example, is the unsuccessful ploy of the doctrine of "Anonymous Christianity," i.e., the teaching that basically all people are Christian, even though they do not realize it. The Hindu religion game uses a similar ploy. It recognizes individual and religious differences, but these are mere illusion compared to the one true liberation in which all differences are dissolved in the monochromatic divine reality.

Finally, the pragmatic world, and hence pragmatic faith, is characterized by "relatedness," as well as by novelty and diversity. Diverse religions, gods, faiths, moralities, rites, creeds are not to be understood as self-enclosed atomic units existing in isolation one from the other. Here is James's corrective to an overstress on novelty and pluralism: relations are real, just as real as the things that are related.

James wants no part of a religious diversity that turns into hostility. Religious wars have been a bane on human history to our own day. Wars are fought to maintain religious *novelty* (called "heresy" by the orthodox). Wars are fought to maintain religious *diversity*. The warriors forget that religious *relatedness* is just as real as the novelty and the diversity. The pragmatic believer tries to be faithful to the complex character of religious reality. He holds on to his own unique religious identity, thus recognizing *diversity* of beliefs. He is open to religious change and development, thereby doing justice to the novelty that characterizes human experience. But he also knows as well that the relationships between the parts of experience are just as real as the parts themselves; he will not let the sparks generated by the diverse and novel clashes of religions ignite into a conflagration.

To conclude, then, in the religion game American style religious faith is part and parcel of the life of action. It involves living, forced, and momentous decisions, viz., *genuine* options. Anything short of this is a masquerade of faith and not the genuine article. Religious hypotheses, no less than scientific ones, must pass the test of action.

The power of religious faith, in James's view, is its ability to liberate me, to tap springs of action within myself that otherwise would remain dormant and closed. The universe is a friendly place. "Reality," James tells us, "is congenial to the powers which you possess." So there is an observable test of the truth and worth of my religious faith: does it foster the growth and expansion of my powers as a human being? In accomplishing this, genuine faith becomes precious and indispensable to me. It transforms the face of the universe. The world becomes a home for me and not a place of exile. I am at home and life is worth living because my unique powers are in demand. An authentic faith gives me the courage and hope to use these powers, for in a friendly universe they have meaning and sense. This hope and meaning that it brings are justification enough for faith. No further "proofs" are required. The pragmatic test is met when my own life of action is enhanced.

Novelty, diversity and relatedness characterize this friendly universe, and these qualities will be reflected in authentic faith. Indeed, these qualities are the springs of that hope which faith brings. Novelty and change become not threats to religion, but challenges for me to use my unique abilities. And pluralism and diversity in religion are not feared, but welcomed. The world's variety is a source of delight. I am burdened with no obligation to reduce it to unity. Truth, even religious truth, is clothed in many colors. Finally, not only does religious faith bring trust in change and delight in variety, it also gives me a sense of kinship with all other things. The relations between things are equally as real as their differences. But this sense of unity is never a "finished" unity. Novelty and chance remain ineradicably built into the very fabric of the world in which I live. And in such a world, the man of authentic faith is at home.

In this chapter we have been concerned mainly with religious experience in its subjective side. Inseparable from faith is the reality which faith reveals. We will need to turn to the divine dimension of that very same reality which delights in novelty, diversity, and relatedness. These qualities will color the pragmatic meaning of God.

God will be a God *within* experience. This is not surprising. The pragmatic world, as we have just seen, stresses *relatedness* and continuity. There are no sharp breaks in reality. There can be no dichotomy between this world and a God who is "out of this world." Experience and reality are correlative terms. The pragmatic meaning of religious experience examined in the next chapter will prepare us to approach a pragmatic meaning for God.

# FIVE: HUMAN EXPERIENCE AS RELIGIOUS

*What I propose to do is, briefly stated, to test . . . by common sense, to use human standards, to help us decide how far the religious life commends itself as an ideal kind of human activity.*
    *William James,* The Varieties of Religious Experience[1]

*If religious hypotheses about the universe be in order at all, then the active faiths of individuals in them, freely expressing themselves in life, are the experimental tests by which they are verified, and the only means by which their truth or falsehood can be wrought out. The truest scientific hypothesis is that which, as we say "works" best; and it can be no otherwise with religious hypotheses.*
    *William James,* The Will to Believe[2]

*The adjective "religious" denotes nothing in the way of a specifiable entity, either institutional or as a system of beliefs. It does not denote anything to which one can specifically point as one can point to this and that historic religion or existing church. . . . It denotes attitudes that may be taken toward every object and every proposed end or ideal.*
    *John Dewey,* A Common Faith[3]

Religion was very much part of the background of pragmatism's founding fathers. Henry James, Sr., was the leading American disciple

70

of the religious mystic Emanuel Swedenborg; this could not but influence William who was most devoted to his father. George Herbert Mead's father, Hiram, was a minister in the Congregational church. This was an age when philosophy was the preserve of clergymen, and this rubbed off on the young philosophical student John Dewey. Dewey, as a matter of fact, in his first years of teaching used to open his classes with long spontaneous prayers. But as these men matured, the reaction set in. The religious concern remained, but it took a turn away from the confessional and the institutional, and a turn toward the experiential. The quotations at the head of this chapter illustrate the pragmatic insistence on judging religion squarely by its impact on human life and experience. As the title indicates, the focus is on (1) human experience (2) as religious. So we will explore this double theme, starting with the meaning given by the pragmatist to "human experience."

From now on we will talk of *experience* rather than of *reality*. It is experience which is the touchstone of reality. Reality is what can be experienced. Whatever cannot possibly be experienced is unreal. And that goes for all the entities that are alleged to inhabit the religious world. Angels and souls and gods are real only to the extent that they are able to enter the realm of human experience. To put them beyond the realm of all possible experience is to put them beyond the pale of what counts for real. So "experience" is the root gut category in the pragmatic philosophy of religion.

What we experience is *nature*. Hear Dewey:

> It is not experience which is experienced, but nature—stones, plants, animals, diseases, health, temperature, electricity, and so on. Things interacting in certain ways are experience. Linked in certain other ways with another natural object—the human organism—they are how things are experienced as well.[4]

Experience and nature go hand in hand. What we experience is nature, and the natural is all that there is to experience. Religion is no exception. It, too, belongs to that natural world of human experience. Indeed, as we will see, it is one of the ways in which we experience the natural world. *How* are things experienced? One answer: things are experienced religiously. Whence we have the typically American angle on the religion game: human experience as religious.

Note that since religion belongs to the realm of the natural, the pragmatist is not concerned about the supernatural.[5] "Supernatural" has a special meaning here. It is the opposite of "natural." Natural is that which can be experienced, and therefore counts for real. Supernatural is that which lies beyond the pale of all possible experience, and therefore is not real. So obviously the pragmatist cannot be concerned with a "supernatural" religion: by very definition it is unreal. The only genuine religion is part of nature, part of human experience. Nothing else is worth talking about.

This rejection of a "supernatural" world is not, of course, unique to the pragmatists. This view is a product of the Enlightenment and of the rise of scientific consciousness. The religious revolution it implies is shattering. Mankind for probably half a million years had maintained an image of a dual universe, in which the visible natural world drew all its power from a greater unseen, unexperienced (and unexperience-able) supernatural world. The natural world was imagined to spring from and depend on the "Void," the Creative Act of God, Brahman, or "The World of Ten Thousand Things"—the Unnameable Tao. The problem of life for people living in the natural world was to bridge the chasm to the supernatural world, to tap those unseen and unseeable powers upon which they considered themselves so utterly dependent. Whence the shock to human consciousness, at least in the West, when the scientific image became the master paradigm to which all other images—including the religious—had to conform. Science operates totally within the realm of the natural. Its stern decree against dualism completely subverted the traditional religious image of a supernatural universe.

So the shattered image of the supernatural is not unique to pragmatism or to the American religion game. What is unique is pragmatism's effort to reconstruct amidst the ruins a naturalistic home for religion. No more dual universe; no more dichotomy between a world of experience and a world beyond all experience; no more supernature behind the scenes pulling the puppet strings for nature; no more utterly transcendent Absolute to provide the ground for the natural world in which we move and live and have our being. What place, then, for religion in a world which is imaged as one universe, one nature, in a world in which the only reality is that which is accessible to human experience? How reconstruct religion so that the game can be played according to naturalistic rules? These are the questions about religion that pragmatism undertakes to answer.

Nature—and that includes religion with all its works and pomps —is experience. Experience is the operative category. Let us make sure we understand experience in the fullest and richest possible way. Pragmatism takes no narrow positivistic approach experience. Do not look for God to be submitted to laboratory tests. There is more to human experience than was ever dreamed of by the hard-nosed empirical scientist or by the positivist philosopher. Pragmatism's "experience" is not the narrowly defined experience of classical empiricism. Experience, on the contrary, is infinitely rich and complex. It has room for anything that in any way at all is part of nature or that in any way at all enters the realm of the human. Mystical experiences and paranormal phenomena of all kinds including the religious are not considered by the pragmatist to be "supernatural" (even though they are often so designated in common parlance). No, they are natural to the extent that and because they belong to experience. Experience is a world that is as rich as the totality of the human and the totality of nature.

Neither, for the pragmatist, does experience take on the pejorative sense assigned to it by rationalism. Rationalism's world is a return to dualism; experience becomes a low-grade confused kind of knowing—a sort of pale reflection of the really real world where absolute reason reigns. We would be back to that traditional image of nature considered as a poor copy of the supernatural where the action really is. No, pragmatism does not consider people pilgrims of the absolute. Nature is not a place of exile where we await entry to our true and supernatural home. It is nature that is our home; and experience is the sum of all the living, doing, suffering, and creating that goes on in that home. Experience and nature are all that we have. But what more, asks the pragmatist, could we possibly want?

A contemporary philosopher Robert Johann puts it this way:

> Time and the world are no longer preliminaries to the main event; they help constitute it. Time is not simply duration, the continuance of what already exists, a span given to man to prove himself worthy of heaven. Time is the creative process itself, in which the real is coming to birth.[6]

Recall James's world of radical empiricism characterized by change, creativity, and the relatedness of everything to everything else. Change does not make up a second-level world to be compared unfavorably to a divine realm where there is no change. Creative possibilities do not imply that this world is flawed in comparison to a divine realm where there is no new perfection because supreme perfection already exists. Finally, the pragmatist has no place for an utterly transcendent divine Other; the religious is intimately part of the human in a world where every reality including anything divine is intimately related to every other reality. For the pragmatist, this is quite enough.

Dewey puts the matter quite straightforwardly. It is only when religion sheds its load of supernaturalist baggage that it can genuinely enrich the natural world of human experience. Believers and unbelievers alike are mistaken when they identify the religious with the supernatural. It is essential to a genuine philosophy of religion that a distinction be made between *a* religion and *the* religious. Let us see what Dewey means.

What divides believers from unbelievers is the "two world" theory of religion. There is the world of nature, experienced by believer and unbeliever alike. On this world they can both agree. And then there is that mysterious supernatural world, experienced by neither believer nor unbeliever. This world the unbeliever neither sees nor believes. The religious man, however, believes though he cannot see. By a kind of "doublethink" he lives in a supernatural world existing alongside of and behind the natural.

We have come to think, says Dewey, that religion must necessarily inhabit a supernatural world beyond the ken of human experience. Two supernaturalist doctrines in particular seem bound up with religion. First, all religions proclaim faith in some Unseen Power upon which humans depend, and second, religions offer hope of some kind of immortality. Such doctrines can be comforting, to be sure. Immortality is a hedge against the despair we feel in the face of certain death. An Unseen Power is a hedge against human weakness and limitation. The only trouble is that both of these doctrines fly in the face of human experience.

Once the path of experience is abandoned, the way is open for the wildest kind of speculation, and for human divisiveness beyond all reasonable resolution. The dark underside of the history of religions bears eloquent testimony, says Dewey, to the destructive potential of supernaturalist doctrines. Religion's march through history is checkered with religious wars, persecutions, and servile obedience to powers unseen. Once you have *a* religion, you are saddled with a load of arbitrary institutional practices along with incredible and often degrading beliefs. This is not to say that the religious dimension is to be purged from human life. No. Religion needs to be restored to the only world that actually exists—the natural world of human experience. Religion needs to divest itself completely once and for all of that supernatural bag of beliefs and practices that are irrelevant to the religious dimension of human living. Not *a* religion, but *the* religious should be the center of our concern.

Right off, note that Dewey is not talking about what people usually call "religious experience." Sacred music, meditation, a walk in the woods or under the stars can trigger a certain kind of experience called mystical, or transcendental, or religious. Many people on relatively rare occasions do indeed have some such privileged and special experiences. They might even be tempted to call them experiences of God. Dewey rightly points out that the experience itself should not be confused with the *interpretation* of the experience. The fact of the experience itself is beyond doubt. But its interpretation *is* dubious. I cannot be sure that it is due to a direct communication rather than, say, to an organically produced change in the blood-flow to the brain, or to a psychologically induced shift to an alpha wave brain state. Such experiences qualify as naturalistic. However they may be interpreted, they are, after all, human experiences. So they do not fall under Dewey's strictures against religious supernatualism. But Dewey is not concerned with fostering or multiplying the occurrence of such religious experiences. While such experiences may be all very well and good, their status as "religious," i.e., their interpretation, remains up for grabs. They certainly cannot serve as a secure foundation for Dewey's project of restoring religion to the natural realm of human experience. We need to focus, says Dewey, not on *a* religion, but on *the* religious. "The religious" does not refer to "religious experience." To what, then, does "the religious" refer?

For Dewey, "the religious" signifies nothing less profound than the in-depth orientation of my whole human life and experience. Religious experiences, in the narrow sense of the term, come and go. But the religious dimension of human experience affects the totality that is me as I orient myself toward the totality that is the universe. Dewey sees the ideal human life as enriched and interpenetrated with this religious orientation. The religious is to be wed to the whole domain of human experience. *A* religion cannot effect such a profound experiential transformation; rather, the supernaturalist nonexperiential bias of religions tends to set religions against the experiential world of daily living. And religious experiences, while they may be transitory high points in the religious dimension of living that Dewey envisages, do not touch the whole of human living. Life has more "lows" than "highs," and it is during the lows that the religious can be most valuable and precious to me.

What are the qualities of this religious dimension of human experience? Or to put the question behavioristically and pragmatically, what does the religious dimension *do* for me? The religious is one of those "attitudes that lend deep and enduring support to the processes of living." The prayer used by members of Alcoholics Anonymous exemplifies the kind of supportive attitudes of which Dewey is speaking. "Oh God, help me to accept the things I cannot change, to change the things I can, and the wisdom to know the difference."

"To accept the things I cannot change:" this attitude Dewey calls "accommodation." To keep going in life, I have to know when to accommodate. I accommodate to the weather, to inflation, to the alternation of day and night.

"Adaptation" is a second fundamental attitude that fosters human survival and growth. While accepting the things I cannot change (accommodation), I must change the things I can: I must adapt. I need not always accept unpleasant conditions and accommodate myself to them. Often I can do something about them. I can get a part-time job to earn the new stereo I want; no need to accommodate myself to doing without. I can wear an extra sweater on a chilly morning; no need to shiver. We irrigate crops rather than putting up with drought. We build antipollution devices for cars rather than suffer slow suffocation. All this is "adaptation." And so, by accommodation and adaptation to the particular problems of life we survive and grow.

Finally there is a third basic attitude that lends "deep and enduring support to the processes of living." This third attitude Dewey calls "adjustment." "Adjustment" is the transformation of my life bestowed by the religious dimension of human experience. What does "the religious" do for me? It transforms not just this or that particular problem area of living but my whole life-orientation. By *accommodation* and *adaptation,* I meet the *particular* different challenges of daily living. But by *adjustment* I am attuned to the *whole* life game in which accommodation and adaptation are only particular moves. The adjustment conferred by the religious dimension colors every aspect of my experience.

When I accommodate to changing conditions, I am showing a passive submissive attitude. When I adapt to changing conditions, I am showing an active intelligent attitude. The *religious* attitude however, is more fundamental:

> There are also changes in ourselves in relation to the world in which we live that are much more inclusive and deep-seated. They relate not to this or that want in relation to this and that condition of our surroundings, but pertain to our being in its entirety.[7]

A change in *religious* attitude makes the whole world look different because the whole me has changed.

Whatever gives overall sense and meaning to my life, whatever unifies myself in all my activities, whatever puts my unified self in tune with the universe in which it lives, whatever does all these things deserves to be called religious. The religious gives me a sense of my own possibilities, and hence is the basis for hope. The religious gives me awe and reverence for the larger whole which supports me and hence is the basis of strength. These functions do not require the doctrinal and institutional accretions of *a* religion. Religion is what religion does. Wherever and however these functions are found, there we are in the presence of the religious dimension of experience.

This religious dimension is no luxury. Where the religious dimension is lacking, every aspect of my experience suffers. Sunday morning religion is not enough to sustain my daily living in unity, hope, and strength. There are those who lead lives that are unreligious (and this may include the Sunday morning religionists), but they are the worse off for it. The unreligious live solely by "the facts," immersed in the realm of the actual. They are blind to possibilities and ideals, and so their lives are essentially without hope and overall meaning. Unreligious people rely for their achievements upon themselves alone, cut off from nature and from their fellow human beings. And so life is lived without the strength it might draw from the larger whole of which they are a part and from the society which sustains them.

As James pointed out, and Dewey would agree, we are dealing here with imaginative faith, not intellectual proof. I cannot, for example, *prove* a *Universal Whole*. A Universal Whole is an imaginative ideal. The world that I actually observe is not universal but limited, not a whole, but a partial view. Still there is no need to keep my sights lowered to the world of observation. There may be more to life than my observations would ever lead me to dream of. I can, however, let my trust in the ideal of a Universal Whole exercise a unifying power over all my action. I cannot *prove* that I am meant to live in harmony with a social and natural world that is congenial to me. Such harmony is an imaginative ideal. The world that I actually observe is filled with social conflict and natural obstacles. But there is no need to keep my sights lowered to this world of observation. I can draw strength from the ideal of trust in my fellows and in the beneficent powers of nature.

Whatever serves as an overall harmonizing ideal of life—this is religious. Without such enriching all-encompassing ideals, my life would be the poorer. But we must be careful, says Dewey, not to pretend that the ideal is already a reality. Wishing it so does not make it so. My imagination can galvanize my energies, give my life a direction and meaning. Thus I am inspired to try to bring about the harmony and unity that I idealize. The mistake of the religions, says Dewey, has been to turn their ideals into antecedently existing realities. To idealize a supreme unity is one thing. But to say that there actually exists a God who unifies and harmonizes all things is something else again. The supernatural God and finished revelation of religion paradoxically, for Dewey, were not *religious*. The religious dimension is meant to function within experience. It is meant to be the overall orienting compass of my experiential energies, emotions, and actions. Supernatural entities allegedly existing beyond experience fail this functional test. Therefore, they do not qualify as religious.

Dewey constructs his world strictly along naturalistic lines. Only a naturalistic religious myth could possibly work for him. For Dewey, the operative religious myth is faith in intelligence. This faith is religious in quality. It energizes the whole orientation of his life. Professional religionists are right to view this naturalistic faith as a dangerous rival. Hence, their tendency to disparage intelligence is not surprising. But Dewey gives his allegiance to faith in the possibilities of intelligence because it avoids the snares of supernaturalism. It does not direct us to look to some power outside of nature to do for us the work that we are supposed to do. It endows our own powers with a religious force. This religious focus on human beings does not mean that they are turned into egotistical gods. We are isolated from neither nature nor society. Indeed, it is this natural and social environment which sustains us. Here within experience is the field where intelligence operates. For Dewey, the pursuit of intelligent inquiry is the *one thing necessary*. Faith in the possibilities of intelligence confers a hope and strength that is religious in its power.

Just like the faith of the traditional religions, this faith provides the integrating dimension to experience. It is the overmastering myth which holds together, illumines, and directs all the diverse aspects and forms of experience. No more than the traditional religious faiths is this faith subject to empirical verification through this or that immediate experiential evidence. Like all religious faiths, only a lifetime of commitment can bear witness to its authenticity.

This commitment to intelligence pushes me to test the limits of my full potential, but without pushing me over the edge into supernaturalism. The religious dimension transcends the humdrum everyday world, but without transporting me completely out of this world in the manner of the traditional religions. The traditional faiths set me at odds with myself. The secular competes with the sacred for my attention. I must earn a living while feeling vaguely guilty for not thinking more about the abode of heavenly rest. The temporal changing self of pragmatic everyday living keeps one eye on the eternal unchanging divinity existing out of this world. Faith in intelligence heals this split between sacred and secular, without surrendering the field to the secular. It looks "beyond" the everyday, but this "beyond" is also a "within." I can do no better than to cite Dewey's own words:

> A work of art elicits and accentuates this quality of being a whole and belonging to the larger, all-inclusive whole which is the universe in which we live. This fact . . . explains . . . the religious feeling that accompanies intense esthetic perception. We are, as it were, introduced into a world beyond this world which is nevertheless the deeper reality of the world in which we live in our ordinary experience.[8]

The out-and-out secularist has no faith to inspire living at a level beyond merely day-to-day practicality. Only the power of a religious commitment can muster one's energies to live at full potential. The sacralist also fails to tap all the riches of human potential, abandoning fate to nonhuman supernatural powers. Dewey's naturalistic faith in intelligence has the best of both these worlds. Like the sacralist Dewey looks to a world beyond the actual world. And like the secularist, Dewey does not want to abandon the realm of the human. So he commits himself not merely to the secularistic actual world, but to the *possibilities,* the wonders, that human intelligence might be able to effect. It is a profound act of faith in the human.

The human is not something given, either in humdrum secular experience or as a divine gift. The meaning of human is mine to create. Human nature is not finished yet. The story is still in the writing. Dewey's act of faith in the possibilities of human intelligence gives him the courage and energy to write this story. We have not begun to realize mankind's potential. This is because we have not begun to apply the full force of human intelligence to social and moral problems. Intelligence guided by the method of science has transformed our physical environment in ways we never dreamed possible. But here our faith has faltered. We have not had the courage to apply this same intelligence and this same method to our moral and social environments. We do not pretend that physical nature is a "given," fixed for all time and not to be tampered with. Whence we are open to constant improvements, for example, in agriculture, transportation, communication, and manufacturing techniques. But we do often pretend that *human* nature is a "given," fixed for all time, and not to be tampered with. Whence we are closed to the possibility of intelligent inquiry into improvements in the world of values. Scientifically based recommendations, for example, to legalize marijuana, to abolish antipornography laws, or to broaden the penal parole system are blithely ignored. We welcome scientific recommendations for the improvement of physical nature; intelligent inquiry into the improvement of human nature is met with an embarrassed defensiveness.

Dewey stood in awe before the possibilities of human intelligence. He saw that we have in our control an instrument that not only can transform the physical world, but can transform ourselves. This instrument is human intelligence perfected by the methods developed by science. Human intelligence evoked in Dewey a religious awe that provided the foundation and orientation of his whole life. Sustained by a religious faith in this intelligence, people derive the courage to reach out for self-transcendence and transformation, but without abandoning the world of human experience. The possibilities of what we could become if only we dared to use this intelligence for our own transformation and improvement formed for Dewey an imaginative religious ideal. These possibilities form that "world" which beckons to us "beyond this world" in which we actually live. This transcendent world of religious faith "is at the same time the deeper reality of the world in which we live in our ordinary experience." Such is the naturalistic religious faith which moves Dewey. In this view, any turn toward supernaturalism drains from human experience that religious dimension which could permeate it. It is an abandonment of our greatest powers and highest human possibilities. It is a refusal to take responsibility for fashioning ourselves into the persons we could become.

Must the religion game American style be played with such hard-nosed naturalism? Dewey wants to relentlessly cleanse the religious closet of all supernaturalistic entities, dogmas and myths. He showed how this could be done while still retaining the vitality that the religious dimension brings to human living. But is the price perhaps too high? In clearing the religious closet of supernaturalism, has Dewey not in one stroke swept away all the great world religions that have nourished humanity for millennia? After all, the number of people who are inspired to worship at the shrine of human scientific intelligence is relatively few. And even among those whose lives are devoted to science, many find that science is not enough. It is but one part of their lives. For the deeper orientation, the religious ideal that orders all the parts, they turn elsewhere. We return again to the question: which is to be the privileged myth—the scientific or the religious? Dewey neatly answers that the scientific myth has itself a religious force. Is this the last word?

William James has shown, and sociology of knowledge confirms, that Deweyan naturalism is not our only option in the American religion game. Dewey's religious stance is not the conclusion either of a logical chain of reasoning or of a controlled experiment. Dewey's religious myth is the creation of a prelogical, prescientific act of faith. Because of his act of faith in it, the scientific quest makes life worth living for Dewey. The scientific quest, in other words, takes on for Dewey a religious aura. And for Dewey, consequently, other myths must submit to the overriding power of the scientific myth. The scientific myth enjoys this absolute authority not because it is scientific, but because Dewey's act of faith in it has elevated the scientific myth to privileged religious position.

By what right does Dewey worship at the altar of scientific intelligence? This faith is the result of what James would call a "genuine option" on the part of Dewey. It is not a result of logic, but is prelogical. It is not an act of mind, but an act of will. And you remember how James defended the right to make a prelogical act of faith: "a rule of thinking," said James, "which would absolutely prevent me from acknowledging certain kinds of truth if those kinds of truth were really there, would be an irrational rule."[9] There is no logical reason why scientific intelligence should be endowed with religious privilege. But Dewey cannot rationally be denied the right to draw a religious strength and inspiration from the scientific quest. The test of faith, again to quote James, is:

> what works best in the way of leading us, what fits every part of life best, and combines with the collectivity of experience's demands, nothing being omitted.[10]

There is no denying that Dewey's naturalistic faith met this test in his own life, and so there is no denying Dewey's right to live by that faith. Now at last we come to the point. What's sauce for the goose is sauce for the gander: Dewey has no right on the basis of his own act of faith to legislate against other acts of faith that meet this same experiential test!

Dewey tells himself a story about the universe and his place in it. His story about the potential of scientific intelligence forms the basic ideal which orients and guides his life. So too, other religions—even the supernaturalist religions—tell stories in support of the basic ideals by which people orient their lives. Can I prove that my story is better than yours? This is a misguided question. Proof is not the issue. The religious dimension of experience antecedes and underlies the business of thinking and proving and problem-solving that carries me through my day-to-day living. The religious dimension is what makes it worth while for me to bother proving anything else at all. When the religious dimension itself becomes a problem, then it is no longer doing the job. It is not *my* religion, my story, anymore. I have "lost the faith." I need a new story, a new faith, a new conversion of my will by which to orient my life afresh.

Religion is a life-hypothesis. It draws its strength not from proof but from commitment. This commitment, like marriage, is a risk. But the risk is unavoidable. As James so well pointed out, to suspend belief because I do not know how it will work out is to guarantee that it will not work out. Myths exist for the sake of behavior. My whole life is the test of my religious myth. Willing comes before knowing. I believe that I might understand. Dewey's faith in intelligence is no less a matter of willed commitment than is the devout Hindu's faith that Brahman is the underlying reality of all things.

Dewey might well admit this. But he would take vigorous exception to supernaturalism being put on a par with his naturalistic faith. "My myth is better," Dewey would retort. "It doesn't go beyond experience. Faith in the possibilities of intelligence is an *ideal*; it is a source of hope that is truly religious in its power. But an ideal remains an ideal; it is not a *fact*. I don't *know* what intelligence can do; but I *believe* in its potential. My naturalistic faith does not allege that any reality exists which I cannot experience; it remains to be seen what the potential of intelligence actually yields in results. Supernaturalistic faith, on the other hand, creates the fact. Here, faith becomes wishful thinking. This is the mistake of supernaturalistic religions like Hinduism."

"The Hindu," Dewey might go on to say, "is sustained by the religious ideal of a world of liberation, perfection and peace. So far, this is perfectly legitimate. But then the Hindu converts that *ideal* into an antecedent *reality*, pretending that this ideal world already actually exists somewhere. Perfection, liberation and peace: these are Brahman, says the Hindu. Brahman is the underlying reality of all things. Like other supernaturalists, including Christians, the Hindu has converted the ideal into a reality. Not only is this illogical. It is antihuman. If the realm of perfection, peace and liberation are imagined to already exist, then there is no need for us to work for such a world now. Supernaturalistic religion thus relieves an individual from taking responsibility for one's own destiny. It stills our desire to cultivate our own potential. Supernaturalism sins against humanity as well as against logic."

I submit that from Dewey's indictment of religious supernaturalism only one thing follows, viz., that for Dewey supernaturalism simply does not do the job that religion is meant to do. However, it is perfectly conceivable that Hindus or Christians could arrive at their supernaturalistic belief systems using the same logic (or lack of it) that Dewey uses. Further, each system could be shown to have humanistic consequences similar to those that Dewey adduces in favor of his naturalism. The upshot is that both naturalism and supernaturalism could serve the same religious function, enjoy equal logical respectability, and serve similar humanistic needs.

Naturalism is a belief system no less than is supernaturalism. It does not follow from evidence; it precedes the search for evidence. Naturalism and supernaturalism are logically on a par. Supernaturalism can inspire humanistic moral responsibility and concern no less than can naturalism. Works of mercy done for the ideal of Christian love bears this out as does the compassionate Bodhisattva ideal of Buddhism, to cite two examples.

The one substantive point at which supernaturalism parts ways with naturalism is the supernaturalist belief in transcendence. Here the naturalist draws the line. It is an arbitrary line from the point of view of logic, but the naturalist feels it *must* be drawn. Once you allow belief in a realm of reality lying beyond human experience, the lid is off. There is no end to the spawning of every kind of superstition and faddist cult. The American religious scene today gives more than a little credence to this naturalistic fear. Witness Krishna Consciousness, the Divine Light Mission of the Maharaj Ji, Aikido, Zen, Nichiren Shoshu, Transcendental Meditation, Gurdjievianism, The Process, Arica, Dianetics, Scientology, witchcraft, devil worship, voodoo, exorcism, and astrology, to say nothing of the Jesus freaks. Allowing for the prelogical character of all religious myths and belief systems, including the naturalistic, can we really afford to say that in religion anything goes? Does not common sense, if not strict logical consistency, demand *some* stricture on religious myth-making? The naturalist's answer is unequivocal, though somewhat arbitrary: the refusal to consider the possibility of a transexperiential dimension of reality. But the price of accepting this answer is high: the elimination, it seems, of all the traditional great world religions from the religious scene. Can the religion game American style make place for the great world religions? Can one hold on to a belief in transcendence while not losing sight of the American philosophical focus on human *experience as religious.* The next chapter will meet this question head-on in its discussion of "A Pragmatic Meaning of God."

# SIX: A PRAGMATIC MEANING
# OF GOD

*The beginning of the search for God lies in reflection upon oneself. The search for God is intimately connected with the discovery of one's own identity.*

*Michael Novak,* Belief and Unbelief[1]

*The real difference between a believer and a true atheist is that the believer is intuitively certain that there is a dimension to life, whether it be on the personal or on the cosmic level, which escapes precise definition and yet constitutes a web of meaning without which all is absurd. On the other hand, the true atheist calls this intuition wishful thinking and affirms, with what he genuinely feels is mature courage, that indeed the whole of life, at every level, is absurd.*

*J. Edgar Bruns,* The Ecumenist *(May-June 1974)*[2]

*First, then, it is myth-making to start with God. For the only real line on God that we can have is through an intense experience of this world and of our involvement in it.*

*Sebastian Moore,* God is a New Language[3]

The three theologians quoted at the head of this chapter all agree on one thing. If you want to learn about God, start with humanity. We might go further and say with Gregory Baum that every statement about God is really a statement about humanity. Such demystification of language about God is most congenial to the pragmatic *blik* on things. Here is why.

In order to talk sense about religion, we have got to beware of the words we use. Advertisers control us with words. Politicians deceive us with words. Most of all, we use words to deceive ourselves. Words are the culprits. Words are slippery and dangerous. And religious words can be more dangerous than any others.

Our thinking is trapped inside our language. Recall from Chapter One the language myth by which we construct the world we live in. The words we use can become for us more real than the things that the words are supposed to stand for. And again, religious words are the most susceptible to such illusory transformation. The words begin to take charge of me instead of my being in charge of the words. We have got to get control over our religious words, and of the meanings which supposedly lie behind those words. This is why Dewey inveighs against supernaturalism in religion. The "supernatural" is a world beyond all possible human experience. It is a world where words can go wild, where anything goes. Unchecked and uncriticized by human experience, there is no type of religious madness that might not flourish in a supernaturalistic universe. Let us take a closer look at the slippery character of our words. Then we will see how we can bring them under control, and thereby arrive at a pragmatic meaning for the word "God."

A main problem with our religious words is what has been called the Humpty-Dumpty syndrome.[4] "When I use a word," Humpty Dumpty said in rather a scornful tone, "it means just what I choose it to mean—neither more nor less." We forget that words are only symbols, pointers. In and of themselves, words have no meaning. Words are supposed to *refer* to something. But our lazy minds forget about the referent and get fixed on the word. And so if we say the word often enough and keep using it in our conversations, we begin to think we know what we are talking about. We say "God" this, and "God" that, for example, and begin to think that we know all about God.

This mistaking of the word for the reality really messes up our thinking. The American philosopher Alfred North Whitehead calls this mistake the Fallacy of Misplaced Concreteness. The God in whom we live and move and have our being is a far cry from that word "God" we tend to use so lightly and confidently. "Not everyone who cries 'Lord!' 'Lord!' will enter the Kingdom of Heaven," said Jesus. He was attacking the Fallacy of Misplaced Concreteness that we so easily fall into in our religious language.

This mental disease of confusing words with things has long infected the human mind. The Jews of the Old Testament forbade that the name of God be pronounced or even written. Swear words are still "bad:" witness all the flap over Nixon's "expletive deleted" transcripts. By focussing on the word like this, we forget what the word refers to. The word assumes a reality of its own. It tends to mean "just what I want it to mean—neither more nor less." And this is very comfortable. God is reduced to the level of my lazy mind. The reality of God (whatever that might be) becomes imprisoned in the word. And then I myself become prisoner to the word. And then we bandy the words about in the fond belief that we are talking about reality, when as a matter of fact all we are dealing with is the Humpty-Dumpty meanings in our own brains.

Now if the word "God" is like other words—and this is a big "if"—it is supposed to be a symbol pointing to something. It is not real in itself but allegedly refers to something else that is the reality. Now where are we to find the *referent* of the word "God"? Maybe in the dictionary. Let us try the *American Heritage*:

> god (gŏd) n. 1. A being of supernatural powers or attributes, believed in and worshipped by a people; especially, a male deity thought to control some part of nature or reality or to personify some force or activity. 2. An image of a deity; idol. 3. One that is worshipped or idealized as a god. 4. A man godlike in aspect or power. (Middle English *god*, Old English *god*. See *gheu(s)* in Appendix.*) God (gŏd) n. 1. A being conceived as the perfect, omnipotent, omniscient originator of the universe, the principle object of faith and worship in monotheistic religions. 2. The force, effect, or a manifestation or aspect of this being. 3. The single supreme agency postulated in some philosophical systems to explain the phenomena of the world, having a nature variously conceived in such terms as prime mover, an immanent vital force, or infinity. 4. *Christian Science* "Infinite Mind; Spirit; Soul; Principle; Life; Truth; Love." (Mary Baker Eddy). —interj. Used as an oath.[5]

Not much help here, is there? The dictionary approach to meaning will give me a good line on the *customary* use of words. The dictionary travels the well-worn ruts of meaning. The dictionary will never get my thinking out of a rut. It only confirms my highly selective, lazy, preformed, ho-hum habits of mind. God is a "being of supernatural powers," "a male deity," "a being conceived as the perfect omnipotent, omniscient originator of the universe," "a single supreme agency postulated to explain the phenomena of the world." So what else is new?

The dictionary, for example, will never get me to ask whether God is "a being" at all. The very existence of the dictionary confirms the prejudice that a *thing* exists corresponding to every word. The word "God" then sends me looking for some *thing* or *being* called God. And so the dictionary comes up with a list of the various ways that people have conceived of this thing or being named god or God.

This little discourse on dictionaries is really a commentary on the human mind. In the search for meaning, our minds, like the dictionary, get trapped in a closed system. Our thinking is bewitched by words. When asked about the meaning of a word, we tend to point to other words. I can find in the same dictionary the definitions of all the words used in the definition of "God;" and the definitions of all the words used in *their* definitions. Definitions of definitions of definitions—the words in the dictionary go merrily round and round, endlessly referring to each other like some great mutual admiration society. The dictionary—and our minds too if we are not careful—functions as a completely closed system. Between the front and back cover of the book, all the meanings are there, beginning with "aardvark" ("a burrowing mammal") and ending with "zyzzyva" ("any of the various American tropical weevils of the genus *Zyzzyva,* often destructive to plants"). A zyzzyva is a weevil of the genus *Zyzzyva.* A "God" is a deity. Round and round we go in the dictionary and in our heads, bewitched by the great system of language which filters all our thoughts and determines what we are able to see and understand.

A dictionary is doomed to remain a closed system. Are our minds doomed as well? Is there any way to break out of the language system trap? My understanding seems hopelessly tied up with language. What I can *say*, that I can *know*; what I cannot say, I cannot know either. George B. Leonard recounts a striking illustration of the censorship language exercises over thinking.

A woman from Monterey, California, told me of the chain of events that followed her first mystical experience. She was washing dishes one sunny day when she was suddenly overwhelmed with an awesome feeling of bliss, accompanied by the conviction that "we are all one." She hastened to tell her family of the marvel that had come into her life. They were quite upset and insisted that she see a psychiatrist. He, too, was deeply concerned, and soon she found herself in a private mental clinic. From here, it was only a short step to a state hospital.

Up to this point, the woman told me, she continued to insist that in some very real sense we are all one. After a couple of days in the state hospital, however, she decided she had had enough, and stopped making this claim. She was quickly released and has since lived a perfectly normal life, being careful only not to slip up and say that we are all one.[6]

We have a highly developed vocabulary for dealing with mental illness. *That* we can understand. But ecstacy, mysticism, altered consciousness leave those of us who use the English language speechless. Without the words to describe it, we cannot, it seems, understand it. So the ecstatic housewife was dealt with as a patient rather than as a seer. The resources and limits of the English language determined what her family considered to be real and unreal in her experience. This is the import of Dewey's rejection of supernaturalism. Experience is the fundamental category of reality. Nothing, but nothing, counts as real if it is alleged to be absent to experience. Any statement I pretend to make about God, then, is to be at the same time a statement about human experience. Otherwise my words, however real they may sound, are hollow. Without rooting in experience, my words are mere fictions floating the stratosphere of empty abstraction. So we do not look to the word "God" to determine the meaning of God. Rather we look to what the word "God" *refers to*, or better, *does* in human experience.

So in the religious side of life, just as in every other part of life, we must learn to think not words but the *referents* of words, not definitions, but the experiential *functions* actually performed by the things I purport to define. Note that we are still involved in a process world. And a God experientially understood is inevitably part of the process. God, then, is to be understood by what he *does*. Such is the pragmatic functional approach to meaning.

Experience really is all we have. Understand experience in the widest possible sense. As Alfred North Whitehead put it:

Nothing can be omitted, experience drunk, and experience sober, experience waking and experience sleeping, experience drowsy and experience wide-awake, experience self-conscious and experience self-forgetful, experience intellectual and experience physical, experience religious and experience skeptical, experience anxious and experience carefree, experience anticipatory and experience retrospective, experience happy and experience grieving, experience dominated by emotion and experience under self-restraint, experience in the light and experience in the dark, experience normal and experience abnormal.[7]

Here in this experience is God to be found. Logical thinking is but one feeble thread in the experiential life process. If I would know God

I must allow full play to this world that is experience. "Play," "Pure Play;" herein, says Charles Saunders Peirce who with James is known as the Father of Pragmatism, lies the way to God. Dewey gives the clue: look to experience; Peirce gives the method—Pure Play, or what he calls the "Neglected Argument" (the "N.A.").

Here pragmatism verges on mysticism. Leaving scientific logic behind for a while the pragmatist launches out to bathe in the deeper waters of experience in all its endless variety and complexity. This launch into experience is powered not by logic but by Musement (Peirce's rather awkward word for what we might call today "meditation" or "contemplation"). Logic has rules. Musement has no rules; it is the Pure Play of our powers. Scientific logic is purposeful. It seeks to control, dominate, manipulate. Pure Play has no purpose, except perhaps recreation; like the Spirit, it blows where it will; it knows not where it is going or what it will receive. This "agreeable occupation of mind" is governed by "the very law of liberty." It is the polar opposite of daydreaming. Play mobilizes and exercises all our powers. Where logic discriminates, play is all-encompassing. If God lies anywhere in experience, the playful attitude of mind will be open and ready to receive him.

Philosophers and theologians tend to coopt for themselves the "proofs" of God's existence. But the divine dimension of human living is too important to be left to the specialists. This is Peirce's point. If God is what the great religions say that God is, then the top priority of every human life would be to come to know and reckon with God. "God" would join sex, money, and health as a primary area of human concern. No one needs to be a doctor of physiology and psychology in order to engage in sex. It is a part of human living. It comes naturally to experience. The experience is utterly concrete. Theories and instruction, if they distract from the experience, are more likely to harm than help. And money. The most average first grader quickly and readily learns what money is, what we can do with it and what it can do for us, where it comes from, and how we can get more. It is soon a part of human living that comes naturally. No theories of economics are necessary. The experience is utterly concrete. Health. Care of health may take a little longer to learn, but no medical degree is required for the mastery of certain basics like staying in bed with the flu, or not touching a hot stove. Such experiences are utterly concrete, and quickly become a natural part of human living. The same thing goes for each and every person's relationship with God.

The divine is as utterly basic to human life as are the sexual, the economic, and the survival dimensions of living. If this is so, then coming to know and reckon with God is as concrete and experiential as coming to know and reckon with money and the hazards of a hot stove. Coming to know God is no more a matter of philosophy and theology than is coming to know money a matter of the science of economics, or coming to know sex and health a matter of the science of physiology and medicine. The divine is part of human living. It comes naturally to experience. The experience is utterly concrete. Theological theories and philosophical instructions, if they distract from the experience, are more likely to harm than to help.

The "problem" of the existence of God has never been a problem in a country like India, for example. That the divine Brahman is the basic reality of all things is "obvious" to the Hindus. If anything is in doubt, it would be the importance and reality of the world that is revealed to our five senses. The situation is just the opposite in the empirical-minded West. "Show me," says the man from Missouri. *Seeing* is believing. Perception is based on the *visual* model. "I see" is a synonym for "I understand." If God is such an obvious and fundamental part of human living, the Westerner is inclined to ask, why can't I see him? This is the dead end to which the Western hang-up with visual perception leads.

Seeing is not the only way of knowing. There are two kinds of perception, says Alfred North Whitehead, viz., *visual* and *visceral*. The first type, the visual, we are perfectly at home with. Seeing is indeed believing. Through visual perception, an object is presented to me spatially in the immediate clarity of shape and perspective. I ask where is God and what does he look like. From the viewpoint of visual perception I have to answer that God is nowhere to be found, and that I do not know what he looks like. Not very helpful.

But all is not lost. There is another kind of perception that is not visual, but is *visceral*. It is in "the guts." I do not *see*, but nevertheless I *know*. I am intuitively aware. A wife "knows" whether her husband is cheating on her, no matter what the neighbors say. A mother "senses" that something is wrong with her baby, even though it looks perfectly all right to everyone else. I want to be judged by someone who loves me, because only such a person can really understand me. The American judicial system is based on the right of trial before a jury of peers. Peers are "in tune" with one of their own kind. In the slang, they pick up "vibrations." They can perceive *viscerally* things that an outsider limited to *visual* perception would never guess at. Philosophers have been overly intellectual in their prejudice toward visual perception as the exclusive model for determining what we can know and what we cannot know. As we can glean from the above examples, *visceral* perception is also a source of true knowledge. In a way, the visceral mode is superior to the visual.

The visceral mode of knowing is concrete, whereas the visual tends toward abstraction. Precisely because it is so abstract, visual knowing seems clearer and more distinct. I can know, on the visual model, that a piece of cake weighs four ounces exactly. My visceral knowledge about the cake, however, is not so exact. Its attraction that impels me to eat it, its taste and texture as I chew and swallow, how it sits with my stomach, the psychological satisfaction it supplies —all this is visceral knowledge. It is the sympathetic interaction of my whole organism with the whole reality of the cake. This visceral perception of the cake is true knowledge. The fact that I cannot express this visceral knowledge with precise clarity does not make it the less true.

Visceral learning is a case rather of too much truth for precision than of too little. It is a knowing process which is totally involving. Where visual knowledge is selective, visceral is completely immersed in experience. It is not the mind alone that perceives; the whole organism is at work. Without visceral knowledge I would have a shadow life; I could not get through the day. Visual knowledge is simply not enough. I could draw up a set of clear specifications for what I would consider an "ideal spouse," but the lowliest person has a reality far richer and more complex than any list of qualities I could possibly dream up. I will never fall in love with a set of statistics (visual-type abstract knowledge) but with a person. And in loving, I come to know with visceral richness and complexity. Interpersonal knowledge is born not of "visual" dreams, but of "visceral" contact. How much more is this the case when we start to talk about knowledge of God!

Visual-logical "proofs" for the existence of God are bound to fail. But this is not surprising with regard to a reality as rich and complex as God's is supposed to be. There is a far better way to God than the logical. God is not present in the clear visual mode. Logical leaps to an absent God will always remain unconvincing. Though God is not present with abstract clarity, he is present to me in a much deeper and profounder way. The question is not: what is the proof for the existence of an absent God? The question is rather: What do my guts tell me about the God who is even now present and acting?

To answer this latter question I must find a way to tune into the unspoken, confused, rich, complex depths of visceral knowing. This way of opening my depths up to the divine presence Peirce called "musement." It would be self-contradictory to attempt to state in logical terms the results of such musings on the basic course and cause of the universe. Musings are a-logical. They are my organism's way of getting in tune with myself and with all that exists. Musement is like Pure Play, says Peirce. Play moves in spontaneous, not logical, rhythms. When I put my musings into words, I am by that very fact diminishing them. I run the risk of making them appear trivial. Musement—visceral knowledge—contains so much more than words can ever convey. And so it is with these trepidations that, following the suggestion of Peirce, I muse out loud on the basic meaning of the universe and of my life.

Already, that last phrase "the basic meaning of the universe" has a grandiose and hollow ring to it. When I muse to myself about the meaning of things, it is really my own life's meaning that I care about. Different people will muse about such questions in different ways. So there is no reason to expect that another muser would follow the same spontaneous paths that I am about to follow. I find that I cannot let go of the feeling that somehow the whole shooting match must make sense. I will tell you why.

Expanding galaxies and atomic structures, beautiful sunsets and autumn leaves, a baby brightly inquisitive and an old man at peace with himself—I find it impossible to believe that all these are the manifestations of chance and absurdity. Meaning is there. I am in tune with it. Every slightest conversation supposes it. When I get up in the morning, I get up to find and make sense out of my day. In my guts, I pattern, interpret and shape my minutes and hours. I do not do this because it is the logical thing to do. Rather, this sense of attunement is the presupposition of all logic, all action, all hope. Not only do I pattern my life and world, but I find the world patterned. The meaning is there. I feel this intuitively, immediately, viscerally.

To be sure, the death of other people, and the prospect of my own death, shock this sense of attunement. So does pain and failure. There is indeed evil. There is disorder. There is frustration, interference, destruction. My very shock in the face of these evils is a witness to the ineluctable faith I have that there *must* be a meaning underlying it all, that evil is not the last word, that order will prevail over disorder, that my very shocked recognition of disorder is possible only because of the underlying order with which I am in tune.

There is a dimension to life beyond minute-to-minute survival. It is a dimension that makes it possible to go on from minute to minute. I cannot define this dimension precisely. I move in it as a fish moves in water. For the most part, I am as unaware of it as the fish is unaware of water. It is a "web of meaning." Without it, everything else is absurd. This is not wishful thinking. I simply could not bother to draw my next breath if I were not breathing in this meaning. Often, this meaning seems little more than a hope that there is meaning. But the hope itself attests to the meaning. The hope is a way of saying that in spite of all contrary evidence, the meaning will prevail, must prevail. There is no other basis on which I can think or carry on a conversation. Every statement I make is a truth that implies Truth as its measure. However passing and ephemeral I might imagine my life to be, I cannot help trying to create some meaning for it. I cannot help trying to make some sense out of it. The suicide says that this hope in meaning was disappointed. But it seems to me that even the very act of suicide attests that there was a meaning to *be* disappointed.

The meaning I make out of my life is not God. I do not create "God." But the inescapable compulsion I have to create meaning—this compulsion it is that reveals God to me. It all hangs together. The sum is greater than the parts. The sum has to exist somewhere. The sum of the parts is God. I *know* this. I know it so well that I find it hard to be conscious of it. It is like my breathing lungs and beating heart. They are there. I know them in my guts. I know them so well that I am hardly ever aware. The image I have of God may be a far cry from the reality revealed to me by my ineluctable will to meaning. But for all that, I am not the less sure that my heart beats or that there is a transcendent reality revealed by the hope I have that keeps me eating and breathing even though I never reflect why. No supernaturalism here. Such is pragmatism's God revealed in the very heart of experience. In the sense of these musings, the divine dimension makes up the very texture of experience.

This *visceral* faith in "God" will find different *visual* imageries for its expression from culture to culture and from religion to religion. Myth varies from myth as religionists around the world construct their respective universes. Geography and accident of birth will determine to a large extent which visual imagery I adopt to express my viscerally perceived revelation of God. But whatever conceptual form my belief takes, it is no luxury. Musement (to use Peirce's word again) reveals to me that belief in God has a survival value. It was within myself that I found a pathway to God. As Michael Novak says —and Peirce might well agree—"The beginning of the search for God lies in reflection upon oneself. The search for God is intimately connected with the discovery of one's own identity."[8] So it was in the depths of my own subjective thrust toward meaning that I found God revealed. But a God discovered in subjectivity is not a subjective God.

God is not created by myself but revealed in and to myself. The divine dimension that I discover is objectively there. Belief in God is no subjective fairy tale that can be either embraced or rejected with impunity. The act of faith is no subjective untestable whim. Belief in God is viscerally arrived at. And the test of this belief is equally visceral.

True, my will to meaning is a thoroughly personal affair made conscious in a thoroughly personal way—my individual musings. But this will to meaning is controlled and constrained by all sorts of outside factors. My life, my whole process of survival and growth, provides the objective visceral test of my meaning for God. A "God" described in purely subjectivist terms simply does not do the job, to put the matter bluntly and pragmatically. The subjective myth side of religious belief does not destroy the need for objectivity and testing any more than the subjective mythic side of science can dispense with scientific objectivity. A wrong assessment of the workability of rival physical models has quite concrete consequences; from such consequences scientists do learn, and people can suffer. A wrong assessment of the rival theistic versus atheistic religious models of the universe has very definite objective consequences for living; from such consequences people can learn and indeed suffer. However personal the act of religious faith, and however subjective the process of discovering God, I am not free to set aside pragmatic norms of the success or failure that comes from living by this faith. As Whitehead said, "Your character is developed according to your faith. This is the primary religious truth from which no one can escape." As I believe so I act. As I act so I am. Beliefs and actions are inextricably intertwined. I do not have to plan to test my beliefs pragmatically. By their inevitable impact on action, they will reveal themselves for what they are; they will pass or fail.

As with the scientist in the laboratory, so also with the religious person in life, honesty is the indispensible virtue. Or as Whitehead put it, "the primary religious virtue is sincerity." Without such sincerity, faith becomes fanaticism. Such is the danger of so-called "blind faith." Granted, religious faith is blind in that it does not rely for its justification on visual, sensible proofs. But faith cannot afford to be blind to the impact it has upon my character and life. My knowledge of this impact will be visceral and subliminal rather than visual and clear. It is precisely because the impact of religious faith (or lack of it) is so profound that visceral knowledge in all its complexity is required to reveal it. Is my faith really putting me in tune with myself, with others, with the work I do and the recreations I enjoy? Does my faith really serve to orient my life to tap my highest powers, and give me the hope and strength to use them? Such far-reaching effects faith will either produce or fail to produce. Willy-nilly, my life is the pragmatic test of my faith. Required on my part are the honesty and sincerity to discern and evaluate this pragmatic impact.

Dogmas about God and clear conceptions of God do not emerge at the visceral level of knowing. At the visceral level, the divine dimension of my life is as wordless and as fundamental as are self-preservation and sex. Indeed it is even more fundamental than these. The divine dimension of life, i.e., faith in a meaning that is more than myself, provides the reason for me to go on living and the hope to produce more of my own kind. In the face of suffering, failure, and the prospect of certain death, this inarticulate, confused, stubborn conviction of an overall meaning to things keeps me going. Such is the basic life of faith usually unquestioned and perhaps better left unquestioned. Like walking and breathing and driving an automobile, it works better when I do not think about what I am doing. We should all be so lucky.

What the mystics call "the dark night of the soul" comes, and not only to mystics. A crisis of faith at that profound visceral level cuts more deeply than suicide. My own meaning is called into question, to be sure, but only because the meaning of everything is called into question. What is shaken is the divine pillar that underlies that deepest of all instincts—self-preservation. This dark night is not to be confused with doubts about whether to accept this formulation of the creed or that, or about which religious sect is preferable, or which religious morality is to be preferred above others. Such doubts exist at the *visual* level of perception. Compared to the "dark night," these are relatively superficial theologians' games. Only those who enjoy visceral religious security can indulge in the luxury of such visual-type disputations. The pragmatic meaning of God looks first and foremost for its testing to the visceral level of doubt and belief. There lies the cutting edge between belief and unbelief, theism and atheism.

The dark night takes different forms. It can come on like a shattering explosion or a gnawing disease, suddenly or gradually and almost imperceptibly; it may be a passing bout, or lodge as a permanent condition; some succumb and die, others emerge cured and stronger than before, and still others wrestle with this dark night their whole lives long. For William James the attack was sudden and shattering; it lasted two long years; his "will to believe" sent this disease into remission, but never completely banished it from his system.

The crisis of visceral faith struck like lightning for James as he tells us in his classic, *The Varieties of Religious Experience:*

> I went one evening into a dressing-room in the twilight to pro-
> cure some article that was there; when suddenly there fell upon
> me without any warning, just as if it came out of the darkness, a
> horrible fear of my own existence. . . . After this, the universe
> was changed for me altogether. I awoke morning after morning
> with a horrible dread at the pit of my stomach, and with a sense
> of the insecurity of life that I never knew before, and that I have
> never felt since. . . .
>
> In general, I dreaded to be left alone. I remember wondering
> how other people could live, how I myself had ever lived, so un-
> conscious of that pit of insecurity beneath the surface of life.
> . . . I have always thought that this experience of melancholia of
> mine had a religious bearing. I mean that the fear was so in-
> vasive and powerful that if I had not clung to scripture-texts like
> 'the eternal God is my refuge,' etc., . . . I think I should have
> grown really insane.[9]

The crisis reached its climax on February 1, 1870, as James records
in his diary for that day:

> Today I about touched bottom, and see plainly that I must face
> the choice with open eyes: shall I frankly throw the moral busi-
> ness overboard, as one unsuited to my innate aptitudes, or shall I
> follow it, and it alone, making everything else merely stuff for
> it?[10]

It is no light matter to lose grip on the religious dimension of living.
These are no mere intellectual doubts that James is recounting. He is
wounded in the guts. His whole organism is floundering. The crisis is
visceral. The solution had to be visceral as well. The solution had to
involve not merely mind and speculation, but action, will, and the
whole organism. James finally saw this and was able to move toward
a resolution of this religious crisis as he tells us in his diary for April
30, 1870:

> Not in maxims, not in *Anschauungen* [i.e., "contemplations"—
> the *visual* level of knowing], but in accumulated *acts* of thought
> lies salvation. *Passer outre* (Let us go beyond—that is, beyond
> these maxims, let us make a fresh start and not be bound by ab-
> stract rules [a move to the *visceral* level]. Hitherto, when I have
> felt like taking a free initiative, like daring to act originally,
> without carefully waiting for contemplation of the external world
> to determine all for me, suicide seemed the most manly form to
> put my daring into; now, I will go a step further with my will,
> not only act with it, but believe as well; believe in my individual

reality and creative power. My belief, to be sure, *can't* be optimistic—but I will posit life (the real, the good) in the self-governing *resistance* of the ego to the world. Life shall be built in doing and suffering and creating."

This will to believe is not to be understood as a reckless, irrational, existentialist self-affirmation in the face of absurdity. James saw that this subjective need to believe and consequent faith would be worthless if it were not supported by an objective world that was congenial to his powers and needs. Only the kind of world with which his organism could live in tune would pass the pragmatic test. The kind of world which has always "fostered periods of revival," said James, and the "expansion of the human mind" is a world which said to the human being: "The inmost nature of the reality is congenial to the powers which you possess." And for James, a world without God is not a congenial world.

The visceral crisis of meaning is a life and death crisis. Is life worth living at all?

> That life is *not* worth living the whole army of suicides declare,
> —an army whose roll-call, like the famous evening gun of the
> British army, follows the sun around the world and never termi-
> nates. . . . We are of one substance with these suicides, and their
> life is the life we share.[12]

Each one of us, James says, is a candidate for the abyss of senselessness and suicide. If I persist in unbelief, the unbelief that is really belief that life is absurd and the world is hostile, then indeed this belief will be confirmed. If I persist, for example, in the belief that my boss and coworkers are hostile and unfriendly, my belief will be confirmed. It is the same. My unspoken faith is a visceral communication. Close your eyes to the possibility of a personal and friendly universe, or a friendly place of work, and you guarantee for yourself a life in an unfriendly world. But open yourself up to the possibilities of friendship around you, and put yourself in tune with the possibilities of a friendly world; the result will be a revelation of character—the supportive character of friends and the meaningful character of the world. This meaningful and congenial character of the universe, which keeps it from exploding into absurdity and senselessness—this is the character of God revealed in the will to meaning. The test of its truth is pragmatic. Only in such a world supported by such a divine character is it worth going on living. How do I know that my openness to another's friendship is a valid attitude? The revelation of the other's friendship provides the confirmatory test that my belief is a true belief. How do I know that my will to believe that the world has a divine character to it is a true belief? The revelation of hope, support and meaning, i.e., the revelation of the character of God, is the pragmatic proof that my belief is indeed a true one. Such, you recall, is the pragmatic test of truth proposed by James:

> . . . what works best in the way of leading us, what fits every part of life best, and combines with the collectivity of experience's commands, nothing being omitted.[13]

This test is expressed in clear conceptual language. A pragmatic logic is being articulated here. But it is not in such logic that the strength of this proof lies. The pragmatic test of God is an affair rather of living than of thinking, of heart rather than mind, of guts not head, of the visceral not the visual.

This visceral belief in God is the primary datum. It supplies the material upon which philosophical articulation, logical proofs, and theological conceptions of God can work. But the experience of a life lived in a world which is enlivened by a divine dimension will always be more than the words that describe that dimension or the logical proofs of its existence. A teacher will often be impatient with the student who says, "I know what I mean but I can't express it." But such a student is perfectly justified. The nonverbal is judge of the verbal. Suppose I get a good look at a mugger who robbed me. I try to describe him to the police. How hard it is to verbalize exact color of hair, caste of eye, texture of skin, turn of nose, twist of lips, size and build of body. But working with the police artist and the help of my gut knowledge, I can gradually assemble a remarkably accurate likeness as we put together a composite portrait. And if I see the bandit in a line-up, my heart skips a beat in a nonverbal "that's him"—no words necessary.

Such, then, is our recognition of God in the heart of human experience. Now to sum up. The closed system of language, as we saw, leads us round and round in circles. The British linguistic analyst Ludwig Wittgenstein sees us trapped by our language game. Our condition, he says, is like that of a fly trapped in a bottle buzzing round and round. The philosopher's mission is to lead the fly out of the bottle. John Dewey pointed the way out for us, viz., by the path of human experience. Dewey's rejection of supernaturalism need not be construed as a rejection of God. Naturalism is a doctrine which points us toward experience. It is there that God is to be found if he is to be found at all. We must stop seeking the divine in some world that lies beyond all possible experience, where religious talk, however pious-sounding, is empty of meaning because we know not to what it could possibly refer.

Where Dewey pointed the way, Peirce provided the method, viz., "Musement."[14] So often the mind's search for God reaches a dead end because we have such a narrow understanding of the mind's ways of knowing. Perception, superficially, is visual, logical, and clear. But this articulate kind of knowing rests on visceral perception, deeper and richer than the visual, albeit more confused and imprecise. Peirce's method of Musement is an exercise in visceral knowing. There is no predicting whither each one's guts will lead him in his musings on life and death and meaning. By musing as it were out loud, I outlined how my particular visceral reflections seem to lead me to a God revealed in my ineluctable will to meaning.

Where Dewey gives the clue, and Peirce the method, William James presents the *test* for religious faith's validity. Not every faith will "do the job." The test of a true belief is pragmatic and rational. The subjective need to believe is all in vain unless it is supported by an objective world that is congenial to that need. Without such objective support, the alternative is suicide, suggests James. He personally faced this dark night, this stark crisis. No Promethean defiance in the face of an absurd universe would do for James. The pragmatic test for religious belief, like all other beliefs, lies in its consequences for the survival, growth, and control of human life. Theistic faith passes this test; atheistic fails.

True to his Protestant upbringing, the approach of William James to faith is highly personal and individualistic. Such individualism, however, is not endemic to the American style of playing the religion game. In fact, the genius of pragmatism lies especially in the way it makes the social side of human living essential for our understanding of humanity. Religion is no less characterized by this social dimension than is economics, government, or science. So we move to the next section in our look at the American style of playing the religion game. Here we explore in more detail religion as a pragmatic need, but now especially in its social dimension.

# SEVEN: RELIGIOUS DYNAMIC FOR A FUNCTIONAL WORLD COMMUNITY

*Not only military activity has thus brought men of different groups together and held them together by means of a political institution until social integration could take place. Religion has served the same purpose. In Europe . . . Christendom made it possible for men to realize that theoretically they belonged to a single society. But even more compelling than the influence of arms and religious faiths has been the influence of barter and trade and the wealth which they have procreated.*

George Herbert Mead, "Natural Rights and the Theory of
Political Institution."[1]

*If, as Macmurray remarks, the function peculiar to religion is "to create, maintain and deepen the community of persons and to extend it without limit," the suppression of religion does more than wipe out its past shortcomings; it makes genuine human community impossible.*

Robert Johann, The Pragmatic Meaning of God[2]

*The most grandiose of these community ideals is that which lies behind the structure of what was called Christendom, and found its historic expression in the Sermon on the Mount, in the parable of the Good Samaritan, and in the Golden Rule. These affirm that the interests of all men are so identical, that the man who acts in the interest of his neighbors will act in his own interest.*

George Herbert Mead, "Scientific Method and the Moral
Sciences"[3]

We have put the cart before the horse in considering religion as a matter of individual psychology. Of course, individualism in religion is undeniable. A William James has shown that he cannot function as an individual without religion. For James the individual, religious faith called forth a congenial and intelligible world that made life worth living. Religion is what religion does. We have seen that what religion does is serve a personal survival function. Religious faith reveals a God of meaning without whom everything would dissolve into absurdity.

But a religion that seems to serve a purely individualistic function is very suspect to contemporary sensibility. A purely private faith is as chimerical as a purely private existence. We do not understand religion until we see it functioning as a *shared* faith. This is because we do not understand human persons until we see that their human reality is something shared, something that is first and foremost held in common. Pragmatism's understanding of human evolution is profoundly social. As we will see, it is wrong to conceive of society as made up of self-sufficient atomic individuals. Rather, it is because individuals, as human, are born of society that they are enabled, as integral parts of society, to advance its evolution. The evolution of human selves is first and foremost social. Religion performs an essential function in that social evolutionary process that makes possible my life and growth as an individual. It is to the pragmatic social function of religion that we now turn in this chapter on the "Religious Dynamic for a Functional World Community."

Pragmatist George Herbert Mead has done most to articulate the essentially social nature of human selves. We rely on Mead, now, more than on Peirce, James, or Dewey, for our understanding of the social self-process, and of religion's function in this socializing process. So let us examine these two themes in turn: (1) the social genesis of human selves; 2) religion's function in the birth of human community.

## 1. The Social Genesis of Human Selves

In his evolutionary and social understanding of human selfhood, Mead is much closer to, say, Teilhard de Chardin than he is to Descartes. Man is not primarily the lonely thinker of the Cartesian *Cogito, ergo sum*. Rather primacy should be given at this stage of evolution, Teilhard would say, to mankind understood as an organically functioning whole; such, for Teilhard, is the emergence of the noösphere: humanity as a kind of global brain of which individuals are the interacting cells. Mead is in Teilhard's ballpark, but as a behavioristically oriented pragmatist, Mead is less willing to talk about a universal human community until he sees mankind *functioning* as a universal community.

So we will start with Mead's more modest account of how an organism becomes a "self." Note the implied evolutionary approach. I am not born as a ready-made self. I must *become* a self. Selfhood does not reside in some metaphysical principle or soul. Rather, in Mead's behavioristic account, self is what self does. Strictly speaking, I should talk of "selving" (a verb) rather than of "self" (a noun).

Next note well that "selving" is not something that an individual does alone. It takes two—to tango, and to "selve." This insight is at the heart of Mead's radically *social* understanding of human nature. Any human self-process involves the interaction of two or more reflective organism*s* (plural). Distinguish, therefore, an *individual* from a *self* (i.e., from a selving process, which is the only way to talk about a self). The individual reflective organism is a *participant* in social interactions (social acts, Mead calls them); a self, or better, a selving-process or social act, involves more than one individual. An individual organism is intelligible as a human self only by reference to the various social acts in which it is a participant. So I cannot be a self all by myself. A "self," then, in evolutionary and behavioristic terms, *is* a social process of reflective organisms. Do not say "I am a self;" say, rather, "We are selving."

This will become clearer if we go back to what Mead calls the "genesis of the self," i.e., the story of how a human infant organism acquires a self. It is the ability to take the role of the other that distinguishes human organisms from subhuman. This ability to take the role of the other makes it possible for me to participate in those social acts which constitute human selves. I must become the other in order to be myself. The infant cries "Mama!" before it is able to say "I." It cries "Mama" and it knows what Mama will do: she will come running, or start playing, or offer the bottle. Because it can take the role of the other, in this case of Mama, the infant becomes an active participant in the social act of mother-nurturing-child. The infant has placed itself in Mama's shoes and anticipates how she will respond in this social game of mother-nurturing-child. Mama, of course, is a player too. It is her ability to take the role of the infant, to anticipate how the infant will respond—e.g., by giggling, or bouncing, or sucking the nipple—that enables her to play her part in this social act. Because of her interaction with the infant she acquires her mothering identity, her mother-self. And because of its interaction with the mother, the infant acquires its childing identity, its beloved child-self. Note, the self here is social. Together they constitute the mother-and-child selving process. The two individuals involved are participants in the social game; they have differing perspectives on this same social act. But the individual is not the self. The self—i.e., the selving—is the social process constituted by the interacting individuals. And it is their ability each to take the role of the other that enables them to play this social selving game.

Childhood play and childhood games are ways in which children practice at becoming selves. First, at the stage of play, the child takes on different roles in turn. A boy pretends to be astronaut, policeman, Daddy, Kung-Fu, garbageman, Indian. Thus he exercises that unique human ability of getting in the shoes of the other, an ability so necessary to the socialization process by which he acquires a self. Secondly, at the stage of game, the process becomes more sophisticated. Consider a softball game. Charlie Brown standing all alone on the pitcher's mound in the pouring rain cannot be said to have a pitching self. Only through interacting with batter, catcher, infielders, outfielders, umpires, crowd and coaches does a pitching self come into existence. Only by taking the role of and responding to the expectations of my fellow-players do I acquire a pitching self-identity. Softballing is a social selving process in which by taking the role of their fellow players each acquires the social selving identity of the softballing social act, the softball game. To play any position successfully, I must be able to take the role of all the other players simultaneously and to respond to their varying expectations. A first baseman, when the ball is bunted, anticipates that the pitcher will cover first, the catcher will back him up, the batter will run, the umpire will hover over the bag, and so makes the fielding and throwing response to these expectations accordingly. Note that unlike the stage of play, the softball player is not taking the role of others singly and in turn, but has somehow gotten into the varying roles of fellow players simultaneously. The first baseman is interacting now not with one other, but with what Mead calls a Generalized Other, and is thus enabled to respond to their complex expectations, thereby acquiring a rather sophisticated first baseman self. The players together constitute the softballing selving process. No individual player alone has a softball self. Each participant in the game has a differing perspective on the same social act. The ability of each to take the role of the Generalized Other enables them to play and thereby acquire a softballing social self identity.

The childhood game is a paradigm of the social acts that go on in society at large. It illustrates how I am constituted a social self, by taking part in my family game, in nation games, language games, job games, marriage games, and church games. The game metaphor is not meant to imply that these social processes are trivial. After all, it is through such social acts that I become the person that I am. There is nothing trivial about acquiring a self-identity. The game metaphor is simply intended to stress the social, processive, behavioristic, and structured character of the self.

In this pragmatic view of human selves as social, no one is an island. Active relationships with others are no luxury. I do not first exist as an individual human being and then decide whether or not I will interact with others. Rather, I *cannot* exist as a human being except as I interact with others. A self is what a self does. It is only in social acts that the selving process occurs; it is only through social acts that I show my specifically human way of existing. Who am I as an individual? As an individual I must be defined socially. I am that point at which intersect all the social acts I am engaged in. I am the point of intersection of all the social games I am playing. Note that a point by itself has no dimensions, no character. I have as many characters as the games I am playing. Each selving process in which I share gives me a particular face. I am the sum of my games. My self-identity is (or better, my selving identities are) as broad and as rich as all the games I am playing.[4]

So the measure of my character and self-identity is my ability to take the role of the other. Mead favors this rather antiseptic sociological language—"taking the role of the other." We can quite readily, it seems to me, translate this into the language of *love*. "To take the role of the other" means to be able to stand in the other person's shoes; it means I can sympathetically enter into the other's perspective, see the world through that person's eyes, and resonate with that one's hopes, and fears and expectations. "To take the role of the other" means somehow to *become* that other. My ability to become the other is the measure of my ability to share in those social acts that confer life and self identity. Love, then, is the key to growth of community. Growth of community is *identical* with growth of the individuals whose interactions make up and define a community. The self is social. The identity of individuals extends as far as the communities in which they participate. Love (taking the role of the other) makes community possible. Love *identifies* me with all whom I love. Love is the key to growth of community. Love is the key to growth of the individual. These two statements mean exactly the same thing. The self is social. Talk of human individuals is identical with talk of the communities that give human identity to these individuals. Love is not something superadded to the individual. Love is constitutive of individual human identity. "I love, therefore I am." No, better: "I love, therefore *we* are." The self is social.

Love, notoriously, is a vague, romantic, amorphous, emotional, fuzzy idea. Note how, in the pragmatic view, love takes on a definite concrete observable character. Love is what love does. This behavioristic meaning of love is akin to what perennial philosophy called "love of benevolence"—love as doing good for the beloved. Love, for the pragmatist, is a matter of doing. More than action done *for* the other, pragmatic love is action *shared with* the other. This sharing is possible because of my identity with the other. In getting into others' shoes, taking their roles, I can interact with them responsively and sensitively. Their good is my good. Their being is my being. Together we act; together we exist; the self is social, and love defines it and makes it grow.

Maybe, however, we should follow the lead of the pragmatists and avoid using the word "love." The word carries a load of romantic connotations that can distract us from a clear-eyed view of the social *act*—the so-called love act—itself. Quite simply, love is what love does. Sometimes what love does is very precise and limited. In no sense do I "fall in love" with all my fellow players in the social games I play. In no sense do I take the role of the other so completely as, say, a couple happily married for fifty years can stand in each other's shoes. Such complete identification with the other is hardly required for most social acts. If "love," for you, implies such complete identification, then better not use the word. In order to play a social game, I must take the role of the Generalized Other sufficiently for the purposes of the game. The identification with my fellow players is partial and defined by the goal of the game and the role each plays in the achieving of the common goal. For example, to acquire a bus-riding self, I must be able to anticipate the expectations of my fellow player, the bus driver, regarding my paying the fare, moving to the rear of the bus, and avoiding smoking. This sympathetic identification with the bus driver is minimal. It is, however, necessary. A child or a sociopath, incapable of even this minimal role-taking (this minimal love?), cannot play the bus-riding game. How much greater is the identification with the other that is required to play successfully the marriage game! Some selving processes cut more deeply than others. Some social acts engage all my sympathies; others but few. But be they superficial or profound, it is the sum of these social acts that gives me my identity.

Before we consider the part that religion plays in the formation

of a world community (a utopian self?), we need to look more carefully at the dynamics of the social self-process. Every selving process
involves two distinguishable phases which Mead (following James)
calls the "I" and the "Me." The Me is the process as already given,
already established. It is where we're at so far. The Me is the structure that the past has conferred on the present social act. The Me of
my family self-process, for example, of the established routines of
getting up, dressed, toileted, breakfasted, and off to work and school
in the morning. Each player of the family game has his or her role:
one gets the breakfast, another gets the bathroom first, another
rouses the lay-abeds, still another fetches the paper and warms up the
car. Such is the family Me, the family social self in the morning. Past
routines have set the rules. The game is fixed. The structure is clear.
How dull! How deterministic!

It would be a dreary determinism if the Me-phase were the only
dimension of the social selving process. But we know very well that
there is never a dull moment in the family game. Enter now the "I"-
dimension of the social selving process. Social acts involve human
players. And human players are notoriously unpredictable. The rules
of the game (i.e., the Me) may be clear, but there is no telling on any
given day just how the game is going to come out. It depends upon
how the individual players respond. The novel unpredictable responses of the individual players is what Mead calls the "I"-dimen-
sion of the social selving process. Social selves are not static and
ready made. They grow and change. Predictability is laced with creativity. The novel I-responses shake up the established structures of the
Me. The interplay of these two phases of the (social) self, the I and
the Me, provides the dynamic by which selves evolve and grow.

To speak of the Me is to speak of the past causes that have made
us what we are today. It is our past actions that give our present interactions the character they have. This is the deterministic side of the
social self. The Me is an objective viewpoint which sees the social self
as the product of the past. To speak of the "I," on the other hand, is
to see that these past so-called *causes* were in point of fact *choices*.
There were other alternatives that were not chosen. It is our past
choices which give our present interactions the character that they
have today. Such is the social self-process viewed from the point of
view of freedom. The I is the subjective side of the social self in the
process of being transformed by the free choices of the players.

For example, as the weeks and years go by, the morning routines
of the family game become fixed and established. The rules of the
game describe the family Me, the family self as viewed objectively.

Each family member understands these rules; each takes the role of all the others; each is thus able to respond, to play, intelligently and effectively. But the responses need not be stereotyped. The social self demands mutual understanding, to be sure, but it does not involve servile conformity. If Mom is sick one morning, daughter, Peggy, makes the breakfast. Johnny gets his auto license and demands that now *he* warm up the car. The others adjust their responses according- ly, and the rules are changed. Joe needs to take an early bus now that he is going to Junior High School, so Joe, not Dad, gets first rights to the bathroom. Little Melissa has the flu, so Dad, not Mom, drives the other kids to school today. Thus the rules change, the Me takes on new shapes, the social self evolves. It is no denial of freedom to view the self as social. It is no abdication of autonomy to affirm that indi- viduals, under the penalty of madness, inevitably must function in community and can find self-identity only in community. The healthy (social) self is the one whose individual organic components are high- ly responsive to each other.

Mead's unrelentingly social view of the self challenges head-on the American fantasy of rugged individualism, solitary autonomy, and sacred privacy. This myth permeates our image of the religious self, no less than of the economic and political. This kind of au- tonomy is illusory; such individualism is fantasy. To cultivate such in- dividualism, solitariness, and privacy is to guarantee a vacuum at the center of the self—a self which can only flourish when nourished by sociality. The American myth confuses the organic connectedness of Mead's social self with the coerciveness of authoritarianism. We have been trained to fear openness and sensitivity to others. They are per- ceived as vulnerability to manipulation by others. This, Mead would say, is a completely wrong view. The individuals who make up social self processes are not like chess pieces passively pushed around the board. The dependence of individuals on community is like the depen- dence of the flower on stem and roots. Freedom from the stem is death for the flower. When Americans seek freedom from the influ- ence of others they are seeking the death of their own selves. Such au- tonomy is a chimera. It does not fulfill the self, but empties it. Who was ever freer than the astronauts from the bonds tying us to this earth, and yet who were ever more dependent upon the input, infor- mation, and even commands issuing from this same earth? Every- thing that I am is a gift from those communities from which I derive life and being. My very uniqueness and the freedoms I enjoy are breathed in from these same communities. Mutuality and dependence are sources of strength, not admissions of weakness.

To sign a declaration of independence from sociality is to sign your own death warrant. The leaf apart from the tree like astronauts who have become incommunicado have all the detached freedom of a corpse. There is one major flaw in viewing freedom as freedom from all dependence upon others. The mistake is to see this dependence as a one-way street. Rather it is *inter*dependence and *inter*relationship that go to make up the social self. And this mutual dependence brings mutual gain. By allowing myself to be responsive to the influence and control of others, I gain for myself influence and control over *them*. By withdrawing into the phony freedom of individualism, I render you powerless to affect me; and by the same token, I render myself powerless to affect you in any way. The self is ineradicably social. The search for identity apart from community is a phantom quest.

This view of the self lays to rest the counter-culture's much-touted fantasies of independence. A social self exposes the emptiness of its cliches: "Do your own thing;" "It's up to the individual;" "Everyone must make up his own mind for himself." These cliches rest upon the false supposition that selves, minds, and identities can come into existence and act in lonely isolation. Such fantasies of independence must be healed by the nourishing bonds of community. Here is where religion can serve a profound pragmatic need of humankind today.

## 2. Religion's Function in the Birth of Human Community

William James rightly stressed, as we saw in the last chapter, the profound role that religion plays in the successful pragmatic orientation of an individual's life. Many individuals have a pragmatic need to believe. James showed the crucial role that faith plays even in the *knowing* process. He thereby showed that individuals who have the *need* to believe have every logical *right* to believe as well. Dewey, however, was suspicious of the individualism and the subjectivism that seemed to infect James's approach to religion. James's view of religion, Dewey felt, said more about James and his individual needs than it said about the objective function and validity of religion itself. To overcome such suspicions, we have turned in this chapter to the social and objective functioning of the self, which leads us now to the objective role played by religion in the genesis of the social self. From James's stress on religion's function of serving individual need, we turn now to religion's function in the birth of human community.

the smooth flow of social interaction, and so does the moral genius. What is the difference between them?

All the difference in the world. Or rather we should say, all the difference in their respective worlds. The criminal finds the established world too large a place in which to live. For the moral genius, on the other hand, the established world is too small. The criminal fractures the given order of things. The moral genius strives to make the given order part of something bigger than itself. So the criminal says hate your friends; your fellow citizens are enemies. The genius says love your enemies; make them your brothers. Both are mavericks, to be sure, the criminal in the name of hatred and division, the moral genius in the name of love and greater unity. The criminal lives in a world too big to handle and tries to break it down. The genius sees the fractured world which actually exists and tries to heal the fractured order so that a greater order can come into being.

In an earlier chapter we cited the parallel between scientific myth and religious myth. Here we can point out a parallel between scientific genius and religious genius. The moral genius is like the great scientist who shatters the established modes of scientific thinking by a bold new hypothesis. In the face of dissonant data which just do not fit into current theories, the great scientist constructs a new hypothesis that from a wider perspective integrates this data into the ongoing game, and the scientific world becomes a wider, more unified, and all-encompassing place in which to live. Similarly, the religious genius, in the face of social processes which remain hostile and divisive, constructs from a wider perspective the rules for a new social game. The formerly dissonant social selves are now integrated into the ongoing game. And the human world becomes a wider, more unified and all-encompassing place in which to live.

The criminal enjoys the approval of a narrow subgroup, be it "the syndicate" or fellow conspirators in a bank heist. But society at large remains and will remain the criminal's implacable enemy. The moral genius enjoys the approval of those whose imaginations are captured by the ideal of a wider and more all-embracing community. Their desire is to welcome the established community into their wider more universal game. Both the criminal and the moral genius are enemies to the given order. But where the criminal looks to its dissolution, the religious genius looks to its wider integration and growth.

In Meadean terms, the "I" of the religious genius makes an offer to the warring Me's. If this genius is truly an effective leader, and not a dreamer or a fanatic, the Me's will perceive this as an offer they cannot afford to refuse. Each warring subgroup will be enabled to see that its own interests are best served by joining the other formerly hostile group in a new cooperative game. From the religious stand-point, I can see every other human being as a possible fellow player. The superficial distinctions between us become less important than the fundamental identity. National boundaries are no longer so high that I cannot take the role of the "foreigner." Social distinctions do not blur the fact of human oneness: "I, who am your Lord and Teacher, have washed your feet; you then should wash each other's feet" (John 13.14). We live on one planet, a blue and white ball sus-pended in space. Each one of us for our interests, needs, and very sur-vival, depends on all the others. This one fact of our shared human identity overshadows all the others. Willy-nilly we *are* one. But we do not yet *function* as one. Fratricidal wars as that in Ireland and geno-cidal wars in Africa and Asia bear eloquent testimony to that sad in-comprehension. A *functionally* universal human community remains still an ideal. Religion has a pragmatic service to perform for human survival—to make that ideal universal community into a functional reality. More than anything else religion identifies me with the total humanity of every other person. When the seeds of religion comes to full flower, everyone will realize that the human game is the most im-portant game of all; it is where our most complete identity lies.

So religious faith is more than a matter of private satisfaction and peace of mind. Departing from James's individualism, Mead sees religion performing a universal social function. For James, religious faith was no luxury but a bulwark against suicide and a matter of his individual survival. For Mead, religion is not luxury for mankind, but a matter of universal human survival. A social self operates only as well as each player takes the role of all the others and thus plays the part with sensitivity and responsiveness. And it is religion that en-ables me to take the role of all other human beings precisely in their and my *humanness*. So it is in religion that we see the seeds and dy-namic for a truly universal human social self.

So the religion game American style is innocent of antihuman innuendos often levelled against the various supernaturalisms. The religion game cuts more deeply to the heart of human identity than do other social acts. Narrower social games involve only this or that facet of the human. They are partially involving. The religion game deals with the human as such. It is totally involving.

In summary, then, religion flows from the very nature of what it means to be a human being. Mead shows how human "selving" is a process. I am not born human. Human is something I must *become*. And I cannot bring this off alone. It takes two or more to "selve." I become myself only by becoming the other. The better I am able to take the role of others, the more profoundly and universally human I myself become. The child develops this social self in play and in games. These games prefigure the wider social games that are the stuff of human living.

It is an illusion to imagine myself as a solitary individual ego pitted against the rest of men. Willy-nilly, the self is social. Only one who loses (individual) self, will find (true social) self. My identity as a human being is a gift that others have conferred upon me. This socially given aspect of the self-process Mead calls the Me. But the passive and the given is not everything. I can respond actively and creatively in the social games I play. This unique power of creatively making a difference in society Mead calls the I-aspect of the social self-process.

The religion game involves not just one or other facet of the self. No, in the religion game, I interact with others totally, precisely in their humanity. I take the role of the other not merely, for example, as a potential buyer (the economic game), or as a fellow citizen (the American game), or as a possible mate (the dating game). No, in the religion game, I identify with the other in all that person's humanness. I become the other totally. In this sense, self-identity is the gift I confer upon myself by loving others.

The religion game, then, is the human game par excellence. To play the game well is risky, as the death of Jesus and the prophets testifies. We are a long way from a practically functional human community. In a nuclear world where interdependence is global, human survival seems to demand that we find our way to forming such a human community. Religion, then, as a catalyst for such a community has a survival function for mankind. We must subvert our established thinking which can see no further than national boundaries and cutthroat economics. The human social self transcends these narrow games. It is bigger than any country or any vested economic interest. The human social self is a global organism. My fellow players in the human game cover the planet's whole surface. When I kill any one of them or let them starve, it is part of myself that dies. Religion's highest function according to Mead is to lead me to this universal self; religion shows how my identity is bound up with that of every other person.

Religion's function, then, is to put the question to the actual institutions of society—those institutions that divide person from person thus blinding us to the basic humanity that unites us all. We have been talking here, of course, about religion at its best. Religion often has been coöpted by the very institutions it was meant to challenge, and used as a weapon of divisiveness. So we have seen and still see Catholic pitted against Protestant, Jew against Arab, and Moslem against Hindu. Like anything else, religion can be abused. But when faithful to its own character, religion has a prophetic function which has a survival value for mankind. A religion faithful to itself is not the pawn of the established order, but can be its severest critic. The White House chaplain is in danger of coercing religion into legitimating the established order, however imperfect or even evil such a social order might be. Various Third World "theologies of revolution," on the other hand, show religion in its critical function of challenging the established order in the name of an ideal world community, though, to be sure, these theologies are not without problems of their own.

Religion's pragmatic function does not stop here. There is more to human living than any given secular dream of a humanistic utopia. We can be bewitched and entrapped even by our noblest ideals. No single myth—even one that is humanistic and utopian—deserves to have the last word. We proceed now to examine another pragmatic function of religion in the next chapter: Religious Liberation: Cracking the Secularist Cosmic Egg.

# EIGHT: RELIGIOUS LIBERATION: CRACKING THE SECULARIST COSMIC EGG

*In forcing us to face the distinction between God and the idols, the word "God" performs its greatest service. For this distinction gives us a critical lever on anything and everything in our world that might claim our attention and devotion. . . . To be oriented on money or power or sex, to give oneself without reservation to one's family or job or nation, to devote one's whole being to the pursuit even of such lofty (but limited) values as truth or beauty—or justice—is to develop one or another side of the self at the expense of other potentialities and aptitudes; it is thus to cripple, and in certain respects enslave, oneself. Only an orientation on the Source of all being and value will enable us to remain open to all that exists and all that is good, and thus free to develop and mature creatively. . . . In providing a critical distance from all claims upon us—whether of family or vocation, nation or ideology—it makes possible some objective weighing of their merits.*

*Gordon Kaufman*, God the Problem[1]

*Once an object is conceptualized as a member of a given class, it is extremely difficult to see it as belonging also to another class. This class membership of an object is called its "reality;" thus anybody who sees it as the member of another class must be mad or bad. Moreover, from this simplistic assumption there follows another, equally simplistic one, namely that to stick to this view of reality is not only sane, but also "honest," "authentic," and*

115

*what not. "I cannot play games" is the usual retort of people
who are playing the game of not playing a game, when confront-
ed with the possibility of seeing an alternative class membership.*
                                    Paul Watzlawick et al., Change[2]

*Religion alone gives hope, because it holds open the dimension
of the unknown and the unknowable, the fantastic mystery of
creation that the human mind cannot even begin to approach,
the possibility of a multidimensionality of spheres of existence,
of heavens and possible embodiments that make a mockery of
earthly logic—and in doing so, it relieves the absurdity of earthly
life, all the impossible limitations and frustrations of living matter. In religious terms, to "see God" is to die, because the crea-
ture is too small and finite to be able to bear the higher meanings
of creation. Religion takes one's very creatureliness, one's insignificance, and makes it a condition of hope. Full transcendence
of the human condition means limitless possibility unimaginable
to us.*
                                    Ernest Becker, The Denial of Death[3]

Thus far religion has been pictured in laudatory and rather glow-
ing terms. But the actual history of religion could appear to be rather
a melancholy record of human savagery. Religious wars and witch-
hunts, human sacrifice and degrading rituals, bigotry and racial
hatred characterize the march of religion through human history. "I
despise your feast days," said the prophet Amos speaking in the
name of the God Yahweh. Amos was railing against idolatry. Idolatry is religion in caricature, especially cruel because it often masquer-
ades under religious auspices. In different ages this masquerade takes
different shapes. In its uglier forms today false religion marches
under a nationalistic banner. In its nobler forms, the banner is humanistic. Such are the idols at whose shrines we worship in the twen-
tieth century. God is country—the nationalistic idol. God is humanity
—the humanistic idol. Such idols immure us in a secularistic prison.

In this chapter we focus on the service performed by true religion
in liberating us from the secularistic prison. Such liberation involves
profound change, the type of change called Conversion in the West,
or Enlightenment in the East. So we will examine, first, our idolatrous condition; secondly, the dynamics of human change; and finally
the solution which religion can supply: (1) Idolatry: the Secularist
Prison; (2) Conversion: The Problem of Change; (3) Religious Liberation: Cracking the Secularist Cosmic Egg.

## 1. Idolatry: The Secularist Prison

Idolatry is a theistic kind of expression. There is God, and then there are false gods, says the theist. Idolatry is the worship of false gods. When subjected to the judgment of the one true God, the false gods are found wanting. "I am the Lord thy God," said Jehova, "thou shalt not have false gods before me." Theism cuts more deeply than does religion. Many people will readily confess to being religious: "I am a religious person, although I don't believe in God." A more demanding faith, however, is required to confess: "I believe in God." In the pragmatic view, religion is what religion does. The last chapter reviewed what religion does (or can do) for the building up of world community. Now we say theism is what theism does. What exactly is the pragmatic function of belief in God?

By virtue of faith, the theist enjoys one ability above all that is not shared by the unbeliever—faith makes the theist an excellent idol-detector. This is a most useful pragmatic function that theism can perform. To understand this better, let us get back for a moment to religion. Recall our introductory definition of the religion game. The religious side of man, we said, is directly concerned with what is *ultimately real*. Such an "ultimate" need not be God or go by the name of God. The ultimate is that without which nothing else in my life would make sense. It gives meaning to my whole life and every part of it. It is the one thing I live for. Whatever name I give it, it is the god I worship above all other gods. Now tell the theist who or what your god is, and you will immediately activate the idol-detector. The theist will try to discern whether it is an idol that holds the place of honor in the shrine where you worship. Such is the "idol-detector" function of theism, about which more follows later.

For now, however, let us look at the religion game in its non-theistic form. I am using the word "theism" here in the broadest possible sense. By a theistic religion game, I mean one that focuses on an ultimate which lies beyond ordinary human reality or the ordinary human state. In this broad sense, theistic religion games are centered on the Holy, the *Tao, Nirvana,* God, or Transcendent Reality. Often, however, the religion game centers upon a god whose name has about it a human-centered accent. The name of my god, for example, could have a ring to it that is psychological, like "self-integration," or political, like "the universal brotherhood of man." It will be the contention of this chapter that theistic religion games serve a pragmatic function not matched by the religions whose gods are merely humanistic. We will get around to inquiring whether, when judged by theism, humanism stands accused of idolatry. We will need to examine what an idol is, why it is a false god, and why *pragmatically* idol-detection is a useful skill to acquire.

Thus far in this book the tone we have taken toward naturalism has been very friendly. Dewey showed that the religious side of man is quite compatible with the naturalist's stress on human experience as the only world worth talking about because it is the only one that counts for real. Mead, again in a thoroughly naturalistic way, pointed out religion's pragmatic function as unifier of mankind. And in James's account of faith experience, we see how even a theistic religion game might be accommodated to a naturalistic world view. But this is a hard saying to traditional theisms, East and West, which have pronounced judgments against this-worldly religions. In theistic eyes, secularism has been a false religion. To the Christian evangelist John, the "world" is the enemy. To the Hindu, this world is *maya* or illusion. So we use a theistic wedge to probe the limits of naturalism. Perhaps the real irony is that naturalism fails on *pragmatic* grounds!

Secularism is that naturalistic religion in which "this world" is all there is. After all, this world is the only world that is given in human experience, and what else do we have besides experience? Any meaning that there is comes ultimately from people. They laboriously build up, test, and constantly reformulate scientific mythologies that give them control over their natural environment. They orient themselves toward this-only-world-there-is through philosophical ideologies. Their imaginations evoke values and ideals to guide their actions; these acquire greater force and influence when embodied in religious mythologies. Religious mythologies often talk of God and project a world beyond the human. But the unsentimental eye perceives that these mythological worlds ultimately curve back upon humanity itself. They remain human creations. Though they speak about *other* worlds, they belong to *this* world. This world given in experience is all that there is. The secular is the ultimate. Humanity is the source and the limit of all meaning and value including the religious. It is a hard saying and it requires great courage to face up to it, but the fact remains that humanity remains turned back upon itself. There is no god but the human.

The thorough-going naturalist would cast a jaundiced eye even upon William James's allegedly naturalistic God. This "God" is suspect of being merely a mythological projection of James's need to believe. This God is no creator of meaning, but is rather himself a meaning created by James. But even assuming such reality for the Jamesian God as James was able to impart, his God remains part of this world. God and James had a gentleman's agreement. God remains James's partner in the moral life. He stands by James's side, assisting his goals, and overcoming the evils which James feels must be overcome. Let us assume that James's finite God can logically be said to exist on pragmatic grounds. Or let us say, at least, that James has justified his right to believe in such a God on the principle of his essay "The Will to Believe:"

> a rule of thinking which would absolutely prevent me from acknowledging certain kinds of truth if those kinds of truth were really there, would be an irrational rule.[4]

This Jamesian God himself remains a thorough-going secularist! For the Jamesian God is committed to this-worldly goals, human projects, and secular mythologies. The Jamesian God worships at the secular shrine. Is James's "God" himself guilty of idolatry?

The secularist myth, in any case, makes this world normative and ultimate. Such meaning as there is is humanly-made. The triumph of this meaning is the task of a person alone, or in the case of James, the task of a man with the help of a God who functions as a kind of elder partner in bringing off the secular project. Bertrand Russell in "A Free Man's Worship" gives poignant expression to the spirit of the secular religion:

> Brief and powerless is man's life; on him and all his race the slow, sure doom falls pitiless and dark. Blind to good and evil, reckless of destruction, omnipotent matter rolls on its relentless way; for Man, condemned today to lose his dearest, tomorrow himself to pass through the gate of darkness, it remains only to cherish, ere yet the blow falls, the lofty thoughts that enoble his little day; disdaining the coward terrors of the slave of Fate, to worship at the shrine that his own hands have built; undismayed by the empire of chance, to preserve a mind free from the wanton tyranny that rules his outward life; proudly defiant of the irresistable forces that tolerate, for a moment, his knowledge and his condemnation, to sustain alone, a weary but unyielding Atlas, the world that his own ideals have fashioned despite the trampling march of unconscious power.[5]

In the secularist myth one is condemned to a ceaseless effort to lift oneself out of a grotesque pit of meaninglessness. But the effort is doomed from the start. One has nothing to hold on to but one's own bootstraps. The Promythean projects of science become a conspiracy by which humanity hides itself from itself. The projects are doomed. Over the absurd abyss, science casts a net of meaning. But the senseless abyss remains. The surd will not go away. It simply takes new forms. The secular medicine in curing the old diseases itself becomes the cause of new ones, as witnessed by nature's ecological backlash. Secular humanity turned back on itself suffers from a malaise that is iatrogenic. It holds on to science, to myths of progress, to cosmological theories. But the dying goes on. The secular shrine rests on foundations that are as weak and mortal as human beings themselves. The secular "ultimate" is terminally ill because humanity is terminally ill. As it dies it hears ringing in its ears inexorable nature's mocking words "Physician, heal thyself."

## 2. Conversion: The Problem of Change

However unsatisfying, shaky, and, in the last analysis, pessimistic the secularist myth may be, what alternative do I have if I am to be hard-nosed and honest about the world the way it really is? Optimistic scientific myths about progress in this world and utopian religious myths about salvation in the next try to deaden my perception of reality in all its ugly harshness. The secularist, alas, sees through these myths. To the person who sees the world through secularist eyeglasses, all escape routes are sealed. Indeed honesty demands this. The oases of security to which science or religion would lead us are in truth mirages. The secularist doesn't "play games." Better live, eyes wide open, to the world the way it is, even though I stare at the face of terror. Such is the grim cosmic egg that encloses secular man.

From inside the egg, religious conversion is unthinkable. All other paths are ruled out. Theism is inevitably illusion. "Conversion" means change of world myth. Once inside a given myth, there is no logical way out. The logic of the myth guarantees that I will stay within the myth. The logic of the myth has an explanation for every possible fact, an explanation that stays within the myth. No fact can count against it. Every bit of "evidence" can be shown to be evidence in support of the myth. No logical argument ever converted a secularist to theism, or a theist to secularism for that matter. World views are susceptible to two levels of change, and these must be carefully distinguished. Changes can occur *within* a given myth. This is first-level change. Then there are changes *of* myth; a new myth is adopted, an old one abandoned: this is second-level change or "conversion." We will take a closer look at these two levels of change in order to see how belief systems work, and what is required to change from one belief system to another. How would one break out of the secularist cosmic egg, the secularist belief system? What would be involved in a "conversion" from secularism to theism?

Secularism, like theistic belief systems, is a ready-made, completely given, and self-contained package of concepts. The package comes complete with its understood premises, its method of argument, and the conclusions that follow from the arguments based on the premises. Once I am securely within the system, the system operates to make sure that I stay securely within it. No other systems seem possible or credible. This self-delusive character of belief systems manifests itself in several ways.

First, as we saw in Chapter One, belief systems are in the reality-construction business. This need not cause any problem. If that is what a belief system does—namely, construct a reality—then that is what it does. The problem comes when I am not aware that this is what is going on. The problem comes when I am so hooked by the system that I forget that all it really does is give me *a* reality. The first fallacy inherent in belief systems is that they make me think that the world created by my beliefs is the only real world, the only one possible. The belief system is like the concept package that is programmed into a computer. The computer proceeds to work on it, no questions asked. Once programmed in, that concept package represents the only world there is so far as the computer is concerned. The data are all there. The premises are all there. In the computer's thinking, they are "obvious." These premises present the only way to think. These premises are the only thing to think about.

Like any other belief system, secularism is subject to this first self-delusive fallacy. The "enlightened" secularist is comfortable in his established way of looking at the world. This established way, to the secularist, is the only way. Those who do not accept this—theists, for example—have a warped and benighted outlook. *This* world is all there is. The scientific method is the best way of understanding it. Any data cited in favor of a transcendent reality, another world, receives a this-worldly explanation. Psychology and sociology, for example, have ready hypotheses to show how meaning systems have a human genesis, and how, try as they may, meaning systems cannot have more than a human reference. A transcendent referent is ruled out *in principle*. There is no room for it in the secularist concept package. The secularist program defines the "obvious" only world there is.

This is not to say that the secularist will not engage in religious argumentation or in debates with theists. But it is true to say that secularist-theist argumentation will never be a real locking of horns. A second fallacy inherent in belief systems is that a true and complete picture of the world is best arrived at by working logically. Once again, the computer is the best teacher of how logic can become a dead end. Feed the wrong program, the wrong concept package, into the computer, and it will relentlessly grind out with flawless logic and in complete detail all the ramifications of the wrong answer. This is an example of first-level change—change which occurs within the limits of a particular myth. First-level change is always "more of the same." First-level change exemplifies the wisdom of the French proverb: *Plus ça change, plus c'est meme chose.* This is the stage at which a theory that was once fresh becomes afflicted with rampant scholasticism. Thousands of arguments are offered to bolster it, but the arguments are all but slightly differing versions of the same old thing.

Logic is not enough to achieve a complete and accurate perception of the world. Listen, if you can stand it, to politicians' arguments during election campaigns. You have the conservative concept package, the liberal democratic concept package, and the concept packages of the moderate republicans, the socialists, or the populists. They carry on panel "discussions." They "debate" endlessly on TV. There is no question they cannot answer. There is no argument that they cannot rebut. Every problem, every piece of data or evidence that is offered them is immediately fed into their respective computer packages. And the answers with their bolstering arguments are spewed out ever so predictable, and oh so dully. Though a thousand "different" topics are dealt with, they all turn out to be variants of the same concept package. It is a game without end.

Similarly, the secularist cosmic egg represents a party line. It can handle all arguments, dispose of all data, turn all evidence to its own support. Argumentation can never convert the secularist to a theistic world view. Arguments against such a person's position when filtered through the secularist computer program are marvelously turned into that one's favor. Arguments between true believers only harden each respective position. Each concept package spins out webs of thought that ever more hopelessly entangle the mind into its one favorite way of looking at the world. Such is first-level change.

"Conversion" would be second-level change. Second-level change is change *of* myth. It is not "yes" thinking. "Yes" thinking accepts the concept package as given. "Yes" thinking is the thinking of faith, of the believer in a given myth. Second-level change does not involve "no" thinking. "No" thinking is the thinking proper to logic. This fits; that does not; x follows from y, but not from z. Logic may also be characterized as "why" thinking. The question "why" evokes the answer "because." And all the reasons given keep spinning round and round within the given myth. It has been said that the child spends the first five years of life asking the question "why." This is gathering information. From age 10 to 75 one learns the "because:" one is socialized into the established myths. It is only during the short span of life during the ages of six through ten that one asks the question "why not." It is "why not" thinking that leads to conversion. It is "why not" language that is the language of second-level change.

Why not consider the sun rather than the earth as the center of the universe? said Copernicus, thereby turning mankind's established astronomical myth on its head and converting them to a new myth. Why not a round earth instead of a flat one? asked Columbus, thereby flying in the face of established common sense and converting humanity to see the earth through new mythological eyes. Why not a God? the secularist might ask himself or herself. Why not believe? Why not a dimension to life that transcends the merely human? Why not a meaning that is more than a human meaning? Why not decide to take seriously humanity's teeming millions who claim to somehow have tuned in to transcendence in multitudinous ways? Why not consider that the great world religions are not systematic delusions, but are valid ways of viewing the universe and the meaning of human life?

"Why not" thinking is the language of conversion. As long as the secularist rests satisfied to ask the question *why,* then God, religion, meaning, faith, happiness can all find complete and adequate explanations *within* the secularist myth. The question *why* can never lead one out of one's own myth. It is the hardest thing in the world to escape from the invisible walls of one's own favorite established myth —and at the same time it is the easiest and simplest thing to do. Wittgenstein said it: "What is your aim in philosophy?—to show the fly the way out of the fly-bottle." Confucius put it even more plainly: "The way out is through the door. Why is it that no one will use this exit?" Why not, indeed?

Second-order change, then, is a leap outside of my taken-for-granted world. Instead of buzzing round and round the fly-bottle whose invisible surface curves in on me and holds me in, I pause, stop the endless self-validating logic, and crawl out the bottle opening into a new world. The door is open: I walk out. Such is second-order change. It is easy enough to talk about, but how very rarely it happens. And this is not surprising. I cannot *try* with any success to change in this radical way. The "trying" will always be more of the same old world. It will be like the fly buzzing round and round inside the bottle at faster and more frantic speeds in the effort to find the way out. The harder it tries the more it is doomed to fail. The accelerated speed is change all right—first-order change. The change is merely more of the same. It is like trying to become an atheist by praying harder to God to make you an atheist. It is like trying to become a theist by looking for scientific proofs for the existence of God. The efforts, in each case, stay within the limits of the old game. I play harder, but it is the same old game I am playing. I will never learn what bowling is all about by working harder at my golf swing. Second-level change is likely to be an affront to common sense. It is liable to appear paradoxical and indeed irrational. As a matter of fact, conversion is necessarily irrational. If I truly succeed in switching myths, I have changed my world and with it my rationality. The new rationality must appear to the old as irrational. The inhabitants of my former world will shake their heads and say I have gone bad; or, if they are more charitable they may say that I have simply gone mad.

### 3. Religious Liberation: Cracking the Secularist Cosmic Egg

If conversion is so difficult, irrational, and unpredictable, how is it brought about? More particularly, how is one to escape from the secularist cosmic egg? I am presuming here a plus value for theism over secularism. I am presuming that a life bathed in transcendence is more richly and optimistically lived than is a totally secular life in which wherever we look for meaning we find our own image staring back at us as in a mirror. If one listens to the secular philosophers, themselves, the secularist cosmic egg is a dismal world albeit we are doomed to live there, and therefore have no choice but to face up to it, courageously spurning theistic hopes and illusions. Are we indeed doomed to be turned in forever (until the species inevitably dies) upon ourselves, or is there a way out? Questions like this lead us to yet another pragmatic function served by religion, and specifically theistic religion. We talk now of religious liberation—a human liberation effected by cracking the secularist cosmic egg.

The appeal of religions is above all practical, and it is this goal of liberation more than any other that unites the great world religions. The language that the religions use to express this goal is radical. It is the language of second-order change. Listen to the words: conversion, liberation, salvation, transformation, death and resurrection, escape, breaking the cycle of birth and rebirth. And second-order change, even in nonreligious contexts, is all of these. It is liberation from an old world, it is conversion to a new paradigm; it is a transformation of *Weltanschauungen*; it is a dying to a former universe in order to rise and live in a new; it is an escape from first-order change, from the endless cycle of birth and rebirth—more of the same —to a radically new level of life which is other than reincarnation in the old cycle. It is of theism's pragmatic function as an agent of second-order change that we speak here.

If a God-oriented universe is to serve this function, the "God" in question cannot be a god whose meaning is quite understandable in the conceptual frameworks and imaginative pictures that we construct for ourselves. It is not the god whose name comes readily to the lips. It is not the god of whom one speaks as if of an absent third person. It is not the god of whom one easily says "it is God's will." It is not the god of our chauvinistic slogans, "in God we trust," "for God and country." It is not even the god whose name is lightly bandied about from the pulpit or in our daily prayers. We are just too comfortable with this god so often appealed to in everyday speech and action. This comfortable god appears completely available to us. And indeed because this comfortable god is so readily available, it is child's play for the secularist to zero in on it, and shoot it down.

The comfortable available god is such an easy target because he is the product of humankind's meaning systems; he is a figment constructed by the human imagination. He fits right in! Why he is so available that even the atheist and skeptic can get hold of him. The atheist and skeptic will describe the god who is the construct of the human imagination, and challenge the believer to show otherwise. Once the believer accepts the challenge on these terms, once the believer consents to discuss the available God, then the argument goes round and round at the level of first-order change: always more of the same, but with all chance of conversion to the transcendent God, all chance of second-order change effectively ruled out. If theism is to function as an agent of second-order change, it cannot refer to the available god. The available god is totally embedded in the realm of human meaning shared by secularist and theist alike. Humanly constructed meanings can only be challenged by the unavailable God, the Transcendent One, the inexpressible Ultimate, Yahweh whose name may not be pronounced, the Brahman behind all appearances, the Tao which cannot be spoken.

Belief, then, in a transcendent God cannot be discussed in human terms because the transcendent precisely is a challenge to the ultimacy of humanly constructed meaning. Here is the crunch. This is the crux of the difference between the secularist and theistic world views. If humanly constructed meaning is all there is, then that is the end of it. Discourse goes round and round in human terms. God is god in name only. He is only as real as the human terms invented to describe him. If God is truly transcendent, then no human terms can grasp him. He is unavailable except on his own terms. He is not the creation or expression of human meaning systems, but stands in judgment of them. Thus belief in an unavailable transcendent God cracks the secularist cosmic egg. Try as we may, we will find this God ever eluding our efforts to grasp him. This God is not easily spoken of in the third person. Indeed he is not easily spoken of at all. He is ever present, ever elusive. He is everything we are not. He is the constant reminder that we are not God, and that Ultimate Reality is greater, richer, and more unimaginable than the sum of all possible human meaning systems could ever make it out to be.

Belief in a transcendent explodes one of the silliest, most pretentious, and unconsciously arrogant heresies of modern man, viz., that the state of understanding of the universe that humankind has reached as of today's date is superior to all previous understandings of the universe ever reached in previous ages. Somehow we find it easy to see the conditioned arbitrary and relative character of religious scientific and moral paradigms of previous ages and of cultures foreign to our own. The contemporary paradigm becomes the standard by which the others are measured. We admit that even this measuring stick will someday be replaced, but we cling to the conviction that it is the best one yet, and that other paradigms stand or fall by how closely they approach the contemporary fashion. Belief in a transcendent blasts this arrogant assumption. In principle, no paradigm is ultimate. More than this, in principle no humanly constructed paradigm could ever say all there is to say, or understand all there is to understand. Further still, in principle, the sum of all possible human meaning systems would not, could not, begin to approach the reality and truth that lie at the heart of things.

This view escapes the secularist's lonely despair. True, be it in a thousand or a billion years, the planet is doomed, and with it the human species too. Human meaning, human truth, and human beauty are pathetically perishable and irrelevant. To the believer in the unavailable God, the Transcendent One, this is no cause for despair. Humanity is not God. Universal meaning will survive the death of human meaning, as will universal truth, and universal beauty. To put mystery at the heart of things is not mystification. Mystification, rather, is to think that a given human paradigm or the sum of human paradigms is all there is. Mystification is to worship the false god humankind. Theistic religion enables us to distinguish between mystification and mystery, false gods and the true. In saving us from idolatry it saves us from despair.

The believer, then, that we are talking about is the believer in the Transcendent God, the truly Other. This is not to say, of course, that the believer somehow escapes this world. The believer, like the secular counterpart, must lead a thoroughly mundane existence. Both are aware of finitude and mortality. Both see all too clearly how fragile and precarious are all humanly constructed cultures and meaning systems. To the secularistic, this mortality and fragility is a signal for, at best, courage in the face of despair. Natural evolution courses on blindly indifferent to the hopes and projects of people. Their dreams of justice, freedom, and meaning have no other roots than the pitifully weak efforts that humans can muster, efforts whose results are inevitably destined to be swept away by the rush of time. It is not easy for the secularist to feel at home in such a world. To the believer, on the other hand, the realm of meaning, justice and freedom is not exhausted by the human species. Sure, the impersonal cosmic processes will sweep away one's humanly created values and meanings, but impersonal cosmic process does not form the most fundamental context in which the believer lives. Nor do merely human efforts provide the most fundamental roots for meaning and value. A mysterious but very real, personal Other lies at the heart of impersonal cosmic process. In this personal Other repose also the most fundamental roots of meaning and value, of freedom, truth and justice. So the believer is no stranger in the cosmos, but can truly be at home. The believer's projects are not in the last analysis the object of cosmic indifference; rather they are the personal concern of that mysterious transcendent God.

This is not a "crutch" theory of faith. The crutch theory views religion as truly the people's opium; it is the universal "cop-out;" those too weak or timid to assume responsibility for their own lives hand the reins over to God. God obliges by taking over the decision-making, laying down the rules, transferring humanity's concern to the abode of heaven rather than the abode of earth. But believers who see their world bathed by transcendence need not smoke such opium. Belief in transcendence makes them more responsible, more concerned. Their lives and their decisions take on a dimension and a depth that the secularist cannot share. Secular tasks and secular goals are as great and as small as humanity itself. Humanity is the measure. There is nothing else. And humanity is ultimately doomed, and with the passing, human achievements and creations pass away too. The believer, however, lives in a universe where there is a basic purpose and order surpassing and quite independent of the individual's purposes and concerns. The ultimate measure now is not humanity, but God. In the last analysis human beings and the universe serve the purposes of God, exist for the purposes of God. Believers' lives still rest in their own hands. They still live on this earth, and cannot shift responsibility to God. But their lives are more than their own. Their goals are rooted beyond this world, and beyond themselves. The measure of their "success" is no longer mere self-integration or merely human fulfillment. The fullness of this world includes more than the merely human. It is by discerning the cosmic purpose and orienting themselves to it that they attain their human fulfillment. They become human through responsible surrender to the more than human. As Jesus said, "Whoever seeks to gain his life will lose it, but whoever loses his life will preserve it" (Luke 17:33). By seeking first the kingdom of God, the believer inherits the human kingdom. The believer is not the plaything of cosmic indifference, but is nourished by cosmic love. The believer seeks self-betterment, but the price is surrender to purposes beyond the self. Real fulfillment comes only through detachment from self-fulfillment.

The believer's framework, then, puts into question the ultimate meaning of all human meaning systems. Indeed, to believers no humanly constructed meaning system can have ultimate validity. Their belief is precisely a surrender of a human-centered universe. Humanity is not God, not the ultimate measure of truth or purpose or meaning or value. Belief, then, serves the pragmatic function of freeing them from obsession with themselves and their own projects. The doom that certainly faces all human projects is no longer an ultimate and final disaster, because these projects themselves are not ultimate and final in import. Theistic belief, then, brings freedom for the self by bringing freedom from the self. If humanity is not God, then the death of the human (individual or species) may not be ultimate death. There is a divine perspective, a framework beyond the human. Not being God, I cannot myself adopt this perspective of all perspectives. But I can situate my human life and meaning within the transcendent divine perspective, although precisely as not human it remains mysterious. In this way every possible humanly constructed perspective is relativized. The pressure is off. I need not devote my life to a lonely and foredoomed struggle against death. I need not commit myself to the ultimate triumph of any human meaning system, be it political, scientific, moral, or even religious. They are all as precarious and fragile as humanity itself is precarious and fragile. If they were of ultimate import, this fragility would be cause for despair. But the believer is not trapped, like the secularist, into worshipping at an altar that must ultimately crumble. No humanly constructed altar deserves such worship. Humanity is not God. God is God. To forget this is to fall into idolatry. Whence we have another way of putting the pragmatic function of religious belief: it delivers me from the necessity of worshipping false gods. It frees me from bondage, moves me from slavery into freedom. The money game, the religion game, the politics game, the morals game, the health game, the self-fulfillment game: none of these warrants my ultimate concern. I can close down these idolatrous shrines in peace and without despair. For these humanly constructed gods are not the center of the world. The universe's center lies transcendently beyond the human. And that transcendent reality is the ultimate focus of all meaning, purpose, truth, value and hope. And it is precisely by surrendering to it that I gain that truth and hope and meaning and purpose that no one can take away from me. Even my own death is not an ultimate disaster because my life and death are centered in a purpose that transcends me. So finally, the most radical pragmatic function of theistic belief is liberation from death itself.

This is heady talk: liberation through detachment, detachment even from one's own death. In the next chapter we will bring things a little more down to earth—less of my final death and more about the little deaths that take place day by day. To put it bluntly and prosaically, we will look at how religion can help us survive an economic depression. Religion can make you wealthy in a world that must kiss affluence goodbye.

# NINE: RELIGIOUS
# DETACHMENT: SURVIVING
# IN A SCARCITY ENVIRONMENT

*So America's economic joyride is coming to an end; there'll be
no more cheap, abundant energy, no more cheap, abundant food,
and soon the flow of cheap consumer goods will suffer increasing
disruption and rising prices. Thus far, spoiled Americans have
met each new piece of bad news with disbelief and sometimes out-
rage. There's been a lot of talk about "who is to blame," and
some groups have taken the position that they have been singled
out for unfair treatment. . . . The charges and countercharges
have filled the air, clogged the media, and done nothing at all to
hasten the adjustments of Americans . . . to new ways of life.
The overall assumption has been that each scarcity is temporary.*
Paul Erlich, The End of Affluence[1]

*Forced slavery is rare these days; rather, servitude is willingly
embraced by those eager for wealth and status, though the ea-
gerness may arise less from greed than from the assumption that
what most people seem to want so much must be supremely
worth having. For the sake of wealth, people already well above
the poverty line slave all their lives, not realizing that withdrawal
from the ratrace would immediately increase rather than diminish their wealth. Obviously anyone who finds the full satisfaction
of all his material desires well within his means can be said to be
wealthy; it follows that, except by the truly poor, wealth can be
achieved overnight by a change of mental attitude that will set
bounds to desires. . . . Remember that mind is the king. Of*

*mind is frustration born; by mind is life endowed with happiness and meaning.*

> *John Blofeld,* Beyond the Gods: Buddhist
> and Taoist Mysticism[2]

*Success to me is having ten honeydew melons and eating only the top half of each one.*

> *Barbara Streisand,* Life[3]

Other people die. My grandparents have died. Several of my friends died last year. My children will die some day. So will you. But it is impossible for me to say with the same full awareness and complacency: "I am going to die." And even that statement is not entirely accurate. More precise, still, would it be for me to say: "I am dying." I. Now. Dying. I have a thousand proofs of the fact. The doctor who thumps and taps and listens to my body performs a ritual not far removed from any jungle medicine man's. The medical dials yield up numbers which the doctor solemnly records. However healthy I may be, after the second decade of life on earth what the doctor is recording is my slow demise. There is no way to stem my body's headlong rush toward death. And the doctor knows it. "Physician, heal thyself," I think. "Fit as a fiddle!" I am told. And so we smile and part. The secret pact to deny inevitable death remains inviolate.

So let us keep our dirty secret. I will not try to exorcise it by writing about it. In this chapter we turn instead to the little daily deaths that we can face and often must. Facing death in small doses might help us take a furtive glance at the awful final death. Is it so awful, really? I am not sure. Let us look at the little deaths to find a clue.

## 1. The End of Affluence

"The joyride is over," says Erlich. And indeed it is. The little deaths are already occurring and there is more to come. I am dying to unlimited use of the car. These wheeled legs of mine are being amputated. I am dying to wintertime indoor heat, steady and high, day and night. Are hot showers the next to go? I am dying to choice cuts of meat. Within ten years will there be meat on the table at all? I am dying to booze and premium beer. These calories are empty and what calories I can afford have to count. One newspaper, not two. The TV is broken; leave it off. I am dying to its flickering images and seductive ads. Magazine subscriptions? Let them lapse. Bookstores? I'll go to the library. The voices of journalists are dying away along with the pulp and print enclosed by bright paperback book covers. I am dying to this year's suits and shirts. Make do with last year's and their "funny" lapels. End of the great American dream. Regress, not progress. Exfluence replaces affluence. Death. Failure. Really?

The list could go on of all the things that I am dying *to*. What is my reaction? Unmitigated loss? Grief? Frustration? Despair? To die *to* or to die *for*—which is to be preferred? I am dying for a car with unlimited mileage. I am dying for wintertime hothouse heat. I am dying for steaming juicy cuts of meat, for booze and color television. I am dying for a magazine in my mailbox every day, a newspaper morning and again at night, and a handful of best-selling paperbacks. I am dying for buckled shoes and stylishly cut shirts. Who is the richer? The person who is dying for all these things and does not have them, or the person who is dying to all these things, and no longer wants them. Does the end of affluence mark the beginning of life? Where dying *for* is slavery, dying *to* is liberation.

These little deaths, are they really deaths at all? "In the animal kingdom, the rule is, eat or be eaten; in the human kingdom, define or be defined." So warns psychiatrist Thomas Szasz. What we define as death, we experience as death. The end of affluence, we say. Is this a matter for mourning or rejoicing? Define or be defined. What is affluence? Affluence—I will define it—affluence is being hooked on trifles and superfluities; affluence is addiction, but not to one drug alone. Affluence is being drugged by every color, shape, smell, touch conjured up by the fifty thousand ads that bombard me every year. The end of affluence, then, is the end of addiction. The end of affluence—rejoice, your liberation is at hand! Define, or be defined. Affluence is slavery and the death of freedom. The end of affluence is liberation and the beginning of life.

Do we have a clue here, now, about death. Define or be defined. Affluence, lost, turned out not to be loss at all but liberation and life. What about death, then? Is death a cause for mourning? Death—is it an ending or, perhaps, a beginning? Which way would you have it? Death is the end, we say. So defined, so it is. And so we lament the end. Our definitions become self-fulfilling prophecies. Put the wrong program into a computer, and you will get the answer—perfectly logical and perfectly wrong. The end of affluence wrongly defined is wrongly perceived. So also death wrongly defined as an ending will be wrongly perceived as an ending.

The mythologies and theologies of the great religious traditions correct these misperceptions. Death is not finality. Death has another face. The other face of death is life. Death is at once birth. One dies to be reborn. In the Christian tradition one speaks not of death alone, but of death-and-resurrection. Death is a rebirth. In East and West, the saved are those who are twice born. Dying to the old becomes a birth to the new. By a rough bloody umbilical cut, the infant dies to the warm comfort of its maternal world. But its howl of grief marks the first breath in a new life in a new world greater and richer than it could have imagined before.

From a womb's eye view the fetal departure is an unmitigated loss. It is only across the divide on the other side that the new life is visible. The trouble is that all we have is a womb's eye view of human death. No signals come from across the divide. The other side remains impervious to us. But we need not be totally in the dark. We can take readings from the deaths and bornings that we do see. There is a pattern to be discerned. We will discern more clearly if we keep two things in mind. First, we can be trapped by one dimensional yes/no, either/or thinking; we must keep our minds open to the possibility of both/and; opposites need not exclude one another; indeed they may well imply one another. In the first view, death excludes life. In the second view, death may well be the other face of life. The second thing to keep in mind with regard to these opposites is that both sides are equally real. To fudge on one is to fudge on the other. Let us see what this means.

Resurrection, rebirth, liberation, enlightenment: these words spring easily to the lips of the religious person. Too easily. One way to avoid the stark and awful face of death is to extoll the glories of the resurrection. To so cheapen death is at once to dim any insight into the new life. If I am honest, death will not be romanticized. Let us pursue this further.

Life has a price. It costs. But life is the meaning of life. Life is all there is. So I am glad it costs. The cost is paid in the coin of death, of dying. I cannot cheapen the coin of death without diminishing the quality of life. New life comes only from death fully accepted, fully suffered through. There is loss. There is grieving for the loss. And until the grieving is completed, the new life cannot come forth. Whether I am talking about a lost affluence, a lost life, or a lost ten-dollar bill, the stark fact remains that a loss is a loss, a death is a death. The new life comes only when I have paid the price, accepted fully the death, completed my grieving.

Nothing is free. Life means growth. Growth means change.

Change means dying to the old that the new may be born. Change is provoked by conflict. Something's got to give, i.e., something's got to die. In the face of conflict, there are two types of people in the world, says psychiatrist Thomas Szasz, viz., the seekers and the avoiders. The seeker knows what is wanted and goes after it; if one method does not work, such a person tries something else, motivated by hope of gain. Eyes fixed steadfastly on the "new life" sought, the seeker is ready to pay the price of dying to the old.

Not so with the avoiders. In the face of conflict, they will try to avoid what they dislike rather than go after what they like. In fact, so intent are they on avoiding problems, they do not know what they positively want. They cling to the old even when the old will no longer do. Not desire for gain, but fear of loss motivates the avoider. One is summoned to grow which means to die, but the avoider is not willing to pay the price of this death to the old life. The avoider is fixed in one-dimensional thinking that loss is final, negative and without redeeming value. Hold on to that bird in the hand even though you are suffocating it to death. Plunge your head ostrichlike into the sand even though this stance is suffocating you to death!

What the seeker instinctively realizes, and the avoider does not, is that on the other side of death is life. Life and death are two faces of the same coin. Every choice is an exclusion, a loss. But it is not just a loss, an exclusion; no, every choice is a choice! The choice of excluding the old makes the new life possible. The loss is real, to be sure; the piper must be paid; life through death is no romantic doctrine. The death is really death. But the new life is really life. Both are real. They condition each other. In facing up to the price, suffering through the grief, accepting the loss, I am plunged into the new life with its unforeseen riches and surprises. "He who loses his life will save it," says Jesus.

This paradoxical life-in-death teaching of the great world religions is very unscientific, very "illogical." This is precisely why a religious dimension to life is a pragmatic need. However paradoxical the life-in-death law is, this death-in-life (same thing!) law is absolutely basic. To miss out on this law is to live a half life, a desperate struggle to cling to the old, a foredoomed battle against inevitable death and the inevitable little dyings that precede that death. To miss out on this law is to live the half-life of the once-born, is to resist rebirth, is to close one's eyes to new possibilities and new life.

There could be nothing more practical than this law of rebirth through death. In quite blunt and materialistic terms, this law can bring instant wealth. Economic loss (death) for example, becomes new abundance (rebirth). Death to the unlimited use of the car can be rebirth to my own body's exercise and my own two legs. Death to the chatter of television can bring freedom to hear my own thoughts. Death to booze and pot can be an awakening to nonsedated reality. Death to newspapers and magazines can mean the birth of free time and a free mind. Death to current fashions and fads can open my eyes to clothes that I choose and enjoy. Affluence defines me as a consumer with goals chosen by others and needs dictated by others. What freedom here? The end of affluence can be the end of this drugged and willing slavery. The death of the consumer can be at once the rebirth of the free person. No longer able to satisfy the needs that others say I have, I can awaken to my true needs. Abandoning pursuit of goals set for me by others, I can set about determining new goals for a new life. Viewed this way, economic death marks the birth of free human life. They are two sides of the same coin.

## 2. Mysticism as a Pragmatic Necessity

I am not talking about religion and detachment as a solution for the devastating poverty such as exists in Calcutta and Bangladesh. Too often has such religious opium been used to bewitch the poor into being content with their poverty. A starving man or child has not the time or energy for the niceties of religious worship or mystical prayer. Indeed I have often thought that religion—and morality too—are luxuries in which only the leisured classes can afford to indulge. This puts it too strongly. But even the Hindu religion, whose teaching on detachment from material things is most uncompromising, allows that sufficiency for bodily health is a precondition and first step for enlightenment. Henceforth, when I use the word "poverty" I will not be referring to grinding indigent squalor that is ruinous to human health and dignity.

What is sufficiency and what is excess? To a very great extent, the answer to this question depends on your state of mind. The Queen of England found three million dollars a year insufficient, so she recently asked for and received a million dollar raise in her annual income. At three million dollars per annum, the queen felt poor. She was unable to survive in the style to which she was accustomed. Do we have here a definition of sufficiency and excess? Is poverty a function of custom—"the style to which I am accustomed"? If my present income tripled tomorrow, I would feel rich for a while. But would I soon become "accustomed" to a new style of living, and so poor and even deprived, if I reverted to the income I have today? It looks suspiciously like poverty and wealth, sufficiency and excess, are really a state of one's mind rather than of one's bank account. If this is true, then the path to wealth lies in control of mind rather than in control of money. How much energy, time, and labor do you invest in trying to get money? Would it be better invested in trying to get control of your mind?

To confuse excess with need, then, is illusion. Such illusion the Hindus called *maya*. You miss the boat if you take (mistake) the world of maya for the real world. Lost in the pursuit of false needs, you never come to know or satisfy your real needs. But how hard it is to discern true from false. In America, this means fighting a universal conspiracy backed by millions and billions of dollars to define you as a "consumer." The bad guys want you to consume junk, buy shoddy goods, and eat substances that could harm or even poison you. Against these bad guys are arrayed the good. They are on the side of the consumer. We have *Consumer Reports* magazine, consumer protection agencies, and laws (all too few) to shield the consumer from those who would do harm. But good guys and bad, how do they all look at you? As a consumer! Who am I? A consumer, that's who I am. What must I do in order to be saved? Consume! What are my most basic needs? An endless array and variety of "goods" to be consumed. What is the greatest sorrow in my life? That I do not have enough money to buy all the things I need to be a good consumer, which in America—if you listen to what everyone tells you—is the same thing as being a good human being. Such is the universal conspiracy to keep you confined in illusion, in the world of *maya*.

The first great illusion then, is to misperceive the true nature of wealth, to confuse excess with need, to be duped by the conspiracy that defines you as consumer. A second, and even more enslaving illusion, is the pursuit of status. Here, of course, frustration is guaranteed. However high I climb, there is always someone higher. Like wealth, status, too, is primarily a state of mind. The loser of a World Championship Boxing Match is disappointed and sad. He lost, didn't he? How strange that he should be disappointed in himself. After all, he is the second greatest boxer in the whole world. That's really not bad! It certainly beats me. But we keep clawing and climbing to the ever elusive top of the status heap. It is a sure-lose game. There is no top, and yet at the top is where everyone tells me I should try to be.

"He who stands on tiptoe, totters," says Taoist philosopher Laotzu. Stop reaching. Sink back on your own two heels. Better still, lie down on the ground. It is relaxing down there. There is no competition. Seek status and prestige, and your value depends on the whims of others. But if you are content with yourself, however you happen to be, no one can take that away from you.

The *maya* of the status game blinds me to the status that I really have. Marshall McLuhan put it this way: "Everyone has the best seat!" There is only one you, and no one is in competition for it. In this lies your value. Here is the "status" that no one can take away from you. How sad not to open your eyes to the status that you really have, i.e., that you really *are,* while pursuing an illusory status that you are guaranteed never to attain.

Whence finally we come to mysticism as a pragmatic need. Mysticism is the science of rescuing my mind from the conspiracy to keep it in illusion. At first blush, mysticism and pragmatism could appear as polar opposites. In the usual image, the mystic is withdrawn and other-worldly, the pragmatist outgoing and this-worldly; the mystic unconcerned with practical consequences, the pragmatist always eyeing observable results. There is some basis for this contrast. There are several varieties of mysticism just as there are varieties of pragmatism. Not all mysticisms will serve the pragmatic needs here at issue, viz., *how to* survive the end of affluence, and *how to* find life from death, *how to* regain control of my mind.

Note the "how to." We are looking for a formula, a prescription. The usual definition characterizes mystical experience as ineffable. It is beyond all words and explanations. Well, grant this, then anything goes. Mysticism thereby transports itself beyond all justification or condemnation. It need explain itself to no man, nor submit to any tests of validity or authenticity. The way is open for every kind of bizarre aberration. It is not without reason that in the Western traditions at any rate the established churches have been uneasy with their mystics. And similarly, the ordinary pragmatist has little use for mystical ineffability with its attendant mumbo-jumbo.

So the mysticism that we are talking about will have to be a mysticism that is at home with the world of everyday, the world of observation, and the world of consequences and results. Such a mysticism indeed would be consonant with pragmatism. Where can such be found? Let the pragmatic method point the way. The various mysticisms in spite of all their alleged ineffability are distinguishable one from the other. The test, not surprisingly, is in the consequences. The practice of mysticism can have radically different results for different people. "By their fruits you will know them." We do not, then, accept the common view that the core mystical experience is in every case the same, while only the interpretations of those experiences will vary. Observation tells us otherwise. An idea is nothing but the practical consequences it has for my life. A look at the results of mystical practice will strip away its protective mantle of alleged ineffability. And a look at the results we are trying to achieve will help us define the kind of mysticism that will serve the pragmatic needs of contemporary humankind.

So the pragmatist looks for mysticism without mystification. "Mysticism is the art of union with the divine." Sounds good, but it is not enough. What kind of union? Friendship? Identity? How would I tell the difference? And the "divine"—is it a being that is "really there?" Or is it a Jungian projection of my own spirit? How would I tell the difference? We will soften the definition, then. "Mysticism is the art or experience of union with reality." Again, this is vague enough, and it is hard to quarrel with it. How is this "union" achieved? Am I not already "real" anyway? What in heaven's name is "reality"? Pragmatism will never be satisfied with a definition. It wants a "how to," a *prescription*. Surprisingly, it is the Buddhist mystic who supplies the prescription that the contemporary pragmatist demands.

It is no accident that Zen Buddhism has found such a ready hearing in America. The Buddhist temper is extremely congenial to pragmatism. However unphilosophical Americans may profess themselves to be, their pulses throb in pragmatic rhythms. And when they look to the Buddhist East to nourish the religious spirit, what they find there is pragmatism in a new guise. This is why they like what they find. The Buddha anticipated by some two and one half millennia the pragmatic stress on action, on experience, and on consequences. He instructed his disciples, "Don't accept the authority of the Scriptures; don't even accept my own teachings, without first testing them out for yourself in your own life and by your own experience."

The Buddha focussed not on doctrine, but on deeds, not on definition but on results. His was not a prophetic revelation to be professed but a mystical path to be followed and lived. Impatient with abstractions and speculative questions, he diagnosed the cause of human suffering and need, and urged practical cures. We have mysticism here all right, but mysticism of a very pragmatic variety.

This is not the time to discourse on historical Buddhism. Suffice it to say that the Buddha's approach was that of a physician. He diagnoses a universal human disease: anxiety and unhappiness. He points out the cause of that disease. And finally he prescribes the remedy. It is all down to earth, very concrete, very practical. The first part of this chapter has diagnosed the contemporary etiology of this disease which is as old as mankind. The virus infecting contemporary America is the end of affluence. But if the virus is to flourish, it requires a congenial host organism. Our culture is such an organism. We are used to affluence; we need it; more than that, we are addicted to it. Deprived of our addiction we are suffering withdrawal pangs and all their symptoms. The Buddha called our universal human disease *Dukkha,* anxiety; it flourishes in Americans with their pinched frowns at the spiraling supermarket cash register and their inflation-generated ulcers as they live out their cultural imperatives to compete, conform, consume.

The reason for this disease, the reason that our organisms are so receptive to the virus, the Buddha called *Trishna,* clinging. We cling to affluence. We are addicted to affluence. We do not know how to die. We do not see that the reverse side of death's coin is life. We do not know how to die, and thereby find new life. We have lost control of our minds. The Buddha points out the *how to,* the cure. Our hope for life lies in the practice of a mysticism that is truly pragmatic. It is called *Nirvana.*

*Nirvana* means breathing out, literally; this is an image for the act of "letting go." The cure is the opposite of the disease. If the disease of anxiety is caused by my clinging to material things, the cure for that disease is to "let go" of my addiction to material things. If I can do this, then the end of affluence is not the end of the world for me. I can die to affluence and thereby find the new life that comes when I am freed from that addiction. All this sounds so logical, and yet it is so very hard to bring off. Our sickness seems unto death—a living death of clinging, of unhappy addiction, of walking faster just to stay where we are. It never occurs to us to get off the treadmill, to stop walking, to let go, to just be who we are, have what we have, live where we live.

It is because I do not know how to solve, or better dissolve, this life-problem, that mysticism is a pragmatic need for me. Let us call the mysticism in question *meditation.* Meditation, then, is the *how to* of *nirvana,* the how to of "letting go." It is that pragmatic prescription we have been looking for. As a pragmatist, I ask what happens when the prescription works? The prescription (nirvana) successfully applied results in enlightenment (satori). But, as we will see, nirvana is not goal-oriented. Better not talk of the results of nirvana. Better say that the state of nirvana is characterized by enlightenment. Well, what am I enlightened about? What is it that I see? What is this realization that brings with it happiness and freedom?

What I see is nothing mysterious. Pragmatic meditation, if I may use the expression, helps me develop the art of seeing what lies in front of my nose. A Buddhist passage puts it this way: "See all beings as the Buddha! Hear all sounds as mantra! Recognize all places as nirvana!" In other words, the world is not divided up into good beings and bad, with the good to be sought after and the evil to be avoided: "See all beings as the Buddha!" Sounds are not divided up into beautiful sounds and harsh, with the beautiful to be sought after and the harsh to be avoided: "Hear all sounds as mantra!" Places are not divided up into good places where I am happy and at home and bad places which are alien and ugly to me, with the good places to be sought after and the bad places to be avoided: "Recognize all places as nirvana!" As Marshall McLuhan says, "Everybody has the best seat!" Or as Zen artist Paul Reps says, "Everybody deserves an award for having an original face!"

Pragmatic meditation directs me to the now, to the present, to this unique experienced moment in all its richness. Pragmatic meditation carves a space out of every day during which I pause to get in touch with myself, with what I am seeing, hearing, feeling, smelling, with my thoughts—not thinking, mind you—but watching my thoughts go by. The present is all I have. How often I miss out on the present because my thoughts are anxiously centered on the future. This place is where I am. How often do I miss out on what is before my nose in my concern for where I am going or where I have come from: I am here, not there. Meditation is nirvana-practice. It is dying practice. I let the past and future drop away, that I may experience the fresh new life that each moment brings. I die to what I do not have that I may enjoy the things I do possess.

Pragmatic meditation is thoroughly naturalistic. It leads me away from abstractions, word traps, thought-nets, and directs me to the heart of my own experience. Proofs, theories, arguments, goals— these can all deceive me. They can be labelled true vs. false, good vs. bad, mine vs. yours. With these labels and distinctions come anxiety —that universal human disease. "Mine" has to prevail over "yours." The "good" has to win out over the "bad," and the "true" over the "false." But the concrete experience moment does not invite these anxiety-producing labels and distinctions. What is, is; there is nothing more to say. Once I talk about it I destroy it. Of course, there is a place for thought and myth and theory and distinctions. We saw this at length in Chapter One, "Religion in the Reality-Construction Business." No harm in this, so long as we see the theories and myths for what they are—constructions. Experience is richer than any net of meaning I cast upon it. To this fullness of experience is where pragmatic meditation leads. It is the great demythologizer. In meditation I come to realize that distinctions and labels are not given me by experience. They are my own doing. If they are not to become my own undoing, I must not give them more reality than the experience that they are meant to qualify.

What has just been said may be true, but it is misleading. I really cannot tell you what will happen to you if you meditate, or what you will see or find there, if indeed anything at all. Each person has a particular strain of the anxiety virus, and the meditation cure will doubtless act differently for different people. One common American version of dukkha or "anxiety" is what cardiologists Friedman and Rosenman call "Type A Behavior" exhibited by a majority of American males. This pattern can be observed "in any person who is aggressively involved in a chronic, incessant struggle to achieve more and more in less and less time, and if required to do so, against the opposing efforts of other things or other persons."[4] Life is a battle, the world a jungle; time is an enemy as are other persons and things. "Hurry!" "Compete!" "Control!" These are the Type A person's watchwords. Diametrically opposed is nirvana's injunction to "let go!" "slow down!" "stop and listen!"

There is something paradoxical in urging pragmatic meditation as a way of getting control of your mind. I am in danger of presenting meditation as just one more product in the achieve-compete-consume ballgame. But meditation means breaking with the old game. I do not meditate because of a goal to be achieved; meditation is itself the goal. In meditation I am not going anywhere; in meditation I see that I have already arrived. There is nowhere to go but where I am; wherever I go, there will I be; so there is no hurry! Yes, this is a new game.

So though meditation may be a pragmatic need, it is not undertaken in a narrowly pragmatic goal-oriented spirit. It is something done for its own sake, like true play. Its utility lies in being useless, like a dance or a parade. We are back to Peirce's Musement, which we saw in Chapter Six. It is a deliberate suspension of the ordinary rules of the anxiety game, a mini-vacation I can give myself every day, indeed several times a day. Meditation is not a product like an automobile. It is not even a skill to be perfected by practice, like a good tennis serve (though tennis played in the spirit of Zen is not unimaginable). Pragmatic meditation is a new way of being.

This new way of being is peaceful and peace-giving. Hostilities are temporarily suspended. No competition. The other is not the enemy. I am who I am; I experience what I experience. And no one can take this away from me. This new way of being is free and liberating. No hurry. Time is not the enemy. The past is always past; the future is ever yet to come. The present is all I have, all I will ever have, and no one can take the present away from me. I can throw away my watch.

Throw away my watch? Sit still? Let the phone ring? Let down my guard? These are unthinkable to the anxiety-ridden achiever-consumer. Their very unthinkability is proof that this truly is a change of being. Meditators escape the achieve-or-fail box. Their very non-achieving is all the achieving they need. Meditators escape the hurry-up or be-late box. No clock can take the measure of the timeless present in which they are. Ordinary time does not govern the meditative state any more than it governs the state of sleeping or dreaming. So at night I set the alarm clock to take over the timing of the ordinary world, while I enter the extraordinary timeless realm of sleep. Meditation is likewise a change of consciousness, but deliberate and active, unlike sleep.

Meditation we called a new state of being, a form of play, a different game. The timeless, goalless world of meditation is a never-never land to one immersed in anxiety, addicted to achievement, consumption, and time. But the faithful meditator may begin to ask which really is the never-never land. Reentering the clock world, the competitive ratrace, maybe will seem like the realm of illusion whereas the meditative state is where the experience of reality truly lies.

Meditation is a way of touching the ultimate, of getting in tune with what really counts. To this extent, it deserves the name "religious" and is a manifestation of how religion is not a luxury, but a pragmatic need. This ultimate goes by many names. Some will call it "God," some the "Self," and others—like the Buddhist—will refuse to name it. I cannot tell you what the meditative state will reveal to you, or if it will reveal any "what" at all. Will meditation become a pragmatic need for you? I guess that, too, remains to be seen—by you.

Professor Van Meter Ames was the first to point out the affinities between American pragmatism and Eastern, especially Zen Buddhist, thought.[5] Pragmatism is very much at home with the Buddhist's holistic approach to the world, practical bent, the high value placed on experience, and the naturalism and suspicion of empty speculation. All of these qualities characterize the American style of playing the religion game. Religion, so remythologized, can have great *meaning*. We now conclude with a parting reflection on its *truth*.

# EPILOGUE

*Council of Hell*

Lucifer: *I have summoned you, my cohorts, to this fiery plain of Babylon today by instruction of His Satanic Majesty. Developments over the past decades have shaken the Kingdom of Darkness to its very foundations. Fallen cherubs are questioning their devilish identity and purpose. Others profess not to know what sin is anymore. The continued existence of hell itself has been called into doubt. This is a moment of unparalleled crisis for the whole demonological institution as such. We can't afford to ignore any longer these fears and anxieties. They're not going to go away until we face them. So I urge a frank and open exchange today on these and any other questions that are disturbing you. Tempter, you look like you want to start us off.*

Tempter: *I say that the question of sin is at the root of all our difficulties. If we can't be sure what sin is, how are we going to devise temptations?*

Lucifer: *Any other suggestions for the agenda?*

Old Horny: *I'd like to see a discussion of how the permissive society affects our mission. Is it a matter for rejoicing? Or must we fight it because it is putting us all out of work?*

Imp: *We could take a holiday!*

Lucifer: *Where'd that God damned imp come from?*

Imp: *You guessed it.*

143

Prince of this World: *Rabbis, ministers, and even priests have stolen my script completely with their talk of the goodness of this world. I'm not sure whether they've joined us, or whether I've been mouse-trapped into working for the Kingdom of Light. My staff is totally confused.*

Serpent: *And with the Pill and Women's Lib, what do we do about the Double Standard? Are women going to be judged the same as men? If so, I'll push adultery harder, and not waste so much time getting them to fornicate.*

Father of Lies: *You all are more hung up on sex than our victims. Nothing has changed that much. Dishonesty, self-deception, lies—these have always been our forte and always will be.*

Old Nick: *And money is still the root of all evil. Money leads people to seek their identity in external prestige and position. This leads to pride, to egoism. And where there's ego, there's hell. That's always been our tradition. I agree with the Father of Lies. Things haven't changed all that much.*

Lucifer: *I think now we have more than enough to discuss. Let's start with sin. The Tempter feels the need of a redefinition. What do you say to that, Old Horny?*

Old Horny: *When humans lived in ghetto groups, the taboos and rules of the moral ball game were clear. "The society that plays together stays together." And there was no talking back to that Umpire in the Sky. But the ghettos are gone. Humans have learned that there are many religion games.*

Prince of the World: *Which is why the clergy can't believe their own propaganda anymore. They feel they were duped. They're falling all over each other to deny what they believed before. Now one may aspire to material things and sensual comfort. Now premarital sex is defended as good. Now one may devote one's life to technological progress.*

Mephisto: *What's the Great Umpire's view? That would give us a clue.*

Lucifer: *We're damned to do without him and his clues. You should know that, Mephisto.*

Imp: *I thought the lines were always open from his side.*

The Father of Lies: *Imp, how dare you talk back to Lucifer. At the risk of boring our fiery hordes, may I repeat: Lies, deception—this is our business. Mess up their heads. That's where it's at.*

Imp: *How do we know you're telling the truth?*

Old Nick: *Shut up, Imp. When you're here as long as your elders, you'll realize we have a code: "honesty among thieves"— no lies during Assemblies of the Unholy Brotherhood. The point, Father of Lies, is "what is truth?" Our damned position is that we have no way of knowing for sure. If I can't even count on money anymore . . .*

Old Horny: *We've got to break out of our ghetto thinking. There's a new religion game going on somewhere. It's up to us to find it.*

Mephisto: *A spy mission! Disguises! Emissaries!*

Old Nick: *To those who know the truth. But who are they?*

Lucifer: *We have no choice but to investigate a random sample of humans from all occupations and walks of life. Our exclusive reliance in the past on theologians, philosophers, and clergymen is what has gotten us into this fix. Somewhere we're bound to discover Jesus, Krishna and Guatama Buddha going about in disguise.*

Father of Lies: *They'll give themselves away. They can't stand having their heads messed up.*

Another Imp: *You're right there! We can't!*

First Imp: *Hint! Start looking for us among the C's: the coal miners, the club ladies, and the candlestick makers.*

Other Imp: *Goodbye. Good luck. Don't forget the cake mongers, the cable car drivers, and the clowns.*

First Imp: *Cabbies, cape twirlers, cribbage players, cigarette girls, chess champions, cabaret owners.*

Other Imp: *Try the cinder carriers, the cobra charmers, the cat lovers and carrot-choppers . . .*

Prince of this World: *Blazes! They're gone. If only they'd be serious, we might get somewhere.*

Lucifer: *Perhaps they are.*

First Imp: *And don't forget the clergy!!!!*


As Old Nick asked the Father of Lies (and as Pilate said to Jesus), "What is truth?" And to the case in point, what is the truth about religion? The series of probes just completed into the religion game, I think, shows that the question is neither as innocent nor as simple as it might first appear. We have looked at religion and the religious from many angles, some oblique, some zig-zag and devious, others less so. These varied perspectives have not always been consistent one with another. Which one, then, is true?

In Chapter Three, we saw many reasons why the truth-giving power of religious myth is being called into question in the contemporary world. Old myths often seem out of tune with new realities. Religious myths, as pointed out in Chapter Two, can make us five ways rich. These myths are givers of meaning: they can give us a cosmos, an identity, a hope of salvation, a morality, and a freedom. The problem is that the available myths of the great world religions often just do not seem to be doing the job. The meanings are there, but not the credibility. The truth-force is lacking. This led us in Part Two of the book to make some probes into a remythologizing of the religion game from the standpoint of American pragmatism.

Well, what is to be said of this American myth? Naturalist vs. supernaturalist, atheist vs. theist, pragmatist vs. absolutist: how am I to weigh one against the other? The test of truth proposed (and indeed *presupposed* as the Introduction makes clear) in this book has been the pragmatic test—the true myth is the one that does the job. You are challenged to test your own religion game in the light of your total life, experience, and action. But let us, in conclusion, hint at a deeper and perhaps less dogmatic way of dealing with the truth of religious myths, including the truth of the pragmatic myth about religion.

In China, it is said, when two children have a quarrel about truth, i.e., about who is right, they are taught to play the "pillow game." Each sits down opposite the other, with a square pillow between them. A problem, like a pillow, has four sides and a center. The child places his/her folded hands on side one of the pillow and says, "There is a place where I am right and you are wrong." Then he shifts his hands to side two, saying, "There is another place where you are right and I am wrong." Moving to side three, he says, "There is also a place where we are at the same time both right and both wrong." Next, placing his hands on side four, he says, "And there is a place where neither of us is either right or wrong and the whole things can be forgotton." Finally, cupping his hands in the center of the pillow, the child affirms "There is a center from which all these approaches flow." At the center, the child, as it were, holds the whole problem in his hands. Then moving back from four, to three, two, and one, the child asserts: "Each one of these steps is good." By using this technique, the child does not stay trapped in the narrow one-dimensional world of either-or, right or wrong, black or white. He lives at that unnamed unified center from which all four viewpoints flow. There is a beautiful freedom in living at the center. The child gets up from the pillow game relieved from the need to win (step one), or the fear of losing (step two). He knows other possibilities. He can admit to being partly right and partly wrong (step three). He can even laugh as the whole problem vanishes (step four). After all, he is the center from which all these approaches emanate.

Let the pillow's four corners represent four approaches to the truth of the religion game, each valid in its own way, each having a legitimate role to play in our lives. The pillow's first corner represents the approach of faith. It is the "yes-thinking" of James's will to believe (see Chapter Four). The pillow's second corner represents the "no-thinking" of logic. Out of this corner we listen to Dewey's insistence on an experiential basis for the religious dimension of human life (see Chapter Five). We hear also Mead's voice describing how religion in the rhythms of pragmatic logic can assist in building a functional world community (see Chapter Eight).

But faith and logic are not the only ways to approach either truth or religion. Yes-or-no thinking can give way to yes-*and*-no, the third corner of the pillow. Religious myths transcend ordinary logic when they point the way to life from death, and to freedom born of detachment and loss (see Chapter Nine). Such paradoxical thinking represented by the pillow's third corner leads easily to the fourth. There is a place beyond logic, be it ordinary logic or paradoxical; there is a place beyond words and concepts.

This is the world of Peirce's pure play or Musement; this is the realm of Whitehead's visceral as opposed to visual knowledge (see Chapter Six). Here we experience theism's power to shatter the secularist cosmic egg; this is where conversions occur when we step out of one universe into another: no single human standpoint can be considered privileged and final (see Chapter Eight), no, not even the standpoint of pragmatism. More than that, should we not beware of becoming too complacent about the religion game itself? "God is not religious," writes novelist Walker Percy, a Christian good and true. The great medieval Catholic mystic Meister Eckhart goes further still, denying both God and not-God. "If you see the Buddha, kill him," the Zen Masters teach.

The center of the pillow represents the place where I, the human being, stand. The world is mine to build (see Chapter One), in faith, in logic, in paradox, in pure play.

A snowflake spun out of the high storm
    achieves its perfect form as it falls,
And touching down,
    it dies.

CHAPTER ONE

[1]Gunter W. Remmling in *Road to Suspicion: A Study of Modern Mentality and the Sociology of Knowledge* (Appleton-Century-Crofts, 1967) details the historical genesis of the science called sociology of knowledge, and uncovers its philosophical and its conceptual presuppositions. Remmling comes to grips with serious philosophical issues (such as the relation of sociology of knowledge to metaphysics), issues which we have necessarily slighted in the brief popularized treatment of this book. Our treatment here is most influenced by Peter Berger and Thomas Luckmann, whose book *The Social Construction of Reality: A Treatise in the Sociology of Knowledge* (Doubleday, 1966) clarifies the methodological presuppositions of the science. For an introductory treatment, see Berger's *Invitation to Sociology* (Anchor Books, 1963). Berger focuses on the sociology of *religious* knowledge in *The Precarious Vision: A Sociologist Looks at Social Fictions and Christian Faith* (Doubleday, 1961), in *The Sacred Canopy: Elements in a Sociological Theory of Religion* (Doubleday, 1967), and in *A Rumor of Angels: Modern Society and the Rediscovery of the Supernatural* (Doubleday, 1969). For a critique of Berger's position together with an in-depth study of the relations between sociology and religion, see Ninian Smart's remarkable little treatise, *The Science of Religion and the Sociology of Knowledge: Some Methodological Questions* (Princeton University Press, 1973).

CHAPTER TWO

[1]Sam Keen and Anne Vally Fox, *Telling Your Story: A Guide to Who You Are and Who You Can Be* (Doubleday, 1973), p. 129.

[2]John Dewey, *Philosophy and Civilization*, reprinted in *The American Pragmatists*, edited by M. R. Konvitz and G. Kenedy (Meridian Books, 1960), p. 176.

[3]Ian Barbour, *Myths, Models and Paradigms* (Harper and Row, 1974), p. 124.

[4]As the reader may have gathered, I have been using the phrase "religious myth" in the broadest possible way to signify (1) a belief system by which a community interprets its experience through a commonly held paradigm which could range anywhere from something like the Apostles Creed to Aquinas's *Summa* of theology, (2) models which suggest such beliefs and which give structure and pattern to myth-stories, like the model of a personal creator God over a created world, and (3) myth-stories like the creation narrative of Genesis or the story of Adam and Eve. See Barbour, *op. cit.*, for a detailed account of these various levels of religious discourse. At each level a similar bipolarity shows itself: there is a tension between subjective constructed meaning and objective intractable truth. Since this bipolar tension is my main concern, I have felt justified in speaking of religious myth in the broadest possible sense of the term.

Ninian Smart in *The Phenomenon of Religion* (Herder and Herder, 1972) distinguishes between static religious doctrines or beliefs and active religious myths or stories. In my usage, both are comprised under the category of myth. Both theological tomes and sacred scriptures are ways in which we tell ourselves stories in order to make sense out of experience.

[5]As noted in the first chapter, this author sees the world, including the phenomenon of religion, through pragmatic eyeglasses. No need for the reader to take pragmatism on faith, however. As you read, see how it works. Check it out.

It is misleading to talk of pragmatism in a generic way. Individual pragmatic philosophers do not present a united or monolithic front on anything, least of all religion—which is all the more reason for the reader to consider critically the variety of pragmatism met in this book.

[6]In this account of the functions of religious myth, I have followed the lead of Barbour, *op.cit.* While taking a functional approach to myth (which includes models and paradigms), Barbour stops short of calling them "useful fictions." In this chapter, we bracket the truth question. We are not concerned with whether myths are useful fictions, detailed pictures of reality, or something in between. We do examine what *meanings* they purport to convey.

[7]Rudolf Otto, *The Idea of the Holy* (Oxford University Press, 1958).

[8]The meaning-giving function of the stories we tell ourselves about experience is delightfully explored by Fox and Keen, *op.cit.*

[9]Educators like A. S. Neil and George Leonard as well as psychologists like Abraham Maslow and Eric Fromm give, each in his own way, a religious force to the quest for self-actualization. Such a humanistic and naturalistic alternative to supernaturalism is very congenial to the approach to religion taken by many (but not all) pragmatic philosophers.

[10]Karl Menninger, *What Ever Became of Sin?* (Hawthorne, 1973).

[11]*Ibid.*, p. 48.

[12]Philip Slater, *Earthwalk* (Anchor, 1974), p. 50.

[13]Robert Bellah develops this thesis brilliantly in *The Broken Covenant: American Civil Religion in Time of Trial* (Seabury Press, 1975).

[14]See John Dewey, *The Quest for Certainty* (New York: Minton, Balch, and Co., 1929).

[15]See Mary Douglas, *Natural Symbols: Explorations in Cosmology* (London: Cressett Press, 1970).

[16]Herbert Marcuse, *One-Dimensional Man* (Boston: Beacon paperbound, 1966), p. 123.

*CHAPTER THREE*

[1]Archibald Macleish, *J. B.* (Houghton-Mifflin Co., 1956).

[2]Reprinted in R. T. Roelofs et al. (eds.), *Environment and Society* (Prentice-Hall, 1974), pp. 370-71.

[3]Thomas Szasz, *The Second Sin* (Doubleday-Anchor, 1973), pp. 21, 20.

[4]Ian L. McHarg, "Man: Planetary Disease," in Roelofs, *op.cit.* p. 307.

[5]This is one of the main themes of Joseph Campbell, *Myths to Live By* (Viking Press, 1972).

[6]We should note that Bultmann's demythologizing of biblical myth was positive in its overall thrust. He reinterprets the myths existentially as statements not about the historical physical world, but about humanity's understanding of itself.

[7]See "The Historic Roots of Our Ecologic Crisis," in Roelofs, *op.cit.*, pp. 6ff.

[8]Campbell, *op.cit.*, p. 252.

*CHAPTER FOUR*

[1]William James, "Is Life Worth Living?" in *The Will to Believe and Other Essays* (Dover Publications, Inc., 1956), p. 59.

[2]William James, "The Sentiment of Rationality," *ibid.*, p. 86.

[3]William James, "The Will to Believe," *ibid.*, p. 29.

[4]*Ibid.*, p. 28.

[5]*Ibid.*, p. 24.

[6]William James, "The Sentiment of Rationality," *ibid.*, p. 86.

[7]*Pragmatism: A New Name for Some Old Ways of Thinking* (New York: Longman's Green and Co., 1947), p. 205.

*CHAPTER FIVE*

[1]William James, *The Varieties of Religious Experience* (New American Library Mentor Book, 1958), p. 259.

[2]William James, *The Will to Believe and Other Essays, op.cit.*, pp. xi-xii.

[3]John Dewey, *A Common Faith* (Yale University Press, 1957), pp. 9-10.

[4]John Dewey, *Experience and Nature* (Dover Publications, Inc. 1958), p. 4a.

[5]James does talk approvingly of a supernaturalist view of religion, but I think his *meaning* is in many ways consistent with Dewey's *naturalistic* account of religion which I present here. For both philosophers, religion's significance is bound up with the experience of human living. Neither James, the theist, nor Dewey, the atheist, accepts a God who transcends all possible human experience.

[6]Robert O. Johann, "Philosopher's Notebook," *America* (February 1963), p. 287.

[7]John Dewey, *A Common Faith, op.cit.*, p. 16.

[8]John Dewey, *Art as Experience* (New York: Capricorn Books, 1958), p. 195.

[9]William James, "The Will to Believe," *op.cit.*, p. 28.

[10]William James, *Pragmatism* (Washington Square Press edition, 1963), p. 38.

*CHAPTER SIX*

[1]Michael Novak, *Belief and Unbelief* (New American Library Mentor Book, 1965), p. 66.

[2]J. Edgar Bruns, "Overcoming the Christian's Impossibility to Believe," *The Ecumenist* (May-June 1974), p. 79.

[3]Dom Sebastian Moore, *God is a New Language* (Westminster, Md.: The Newman Press, 1967), p. 93.

[4]Joseph Danysh in *Stop Without Quitting* (San Francisco, Calif.: International Society for General Semantics, 1974), p. 24, has dubbed as the Humpty-Dumpty syndrome our habitual lazy inattention to what the actual referents of words really are.

[5]*American Heritage Dictionary* (American Heritage Publishing Co., 1969), p. 564.

[6]George Leonard, "Language and Reality," *Harper's* (November, 1974).

[7]Alfred North Whitehead, *Adventures of Ideas* (Macmillan, 1933), pp. 290-91.

[8]Novak, *op.cit.*, p. 66.

[9]William James, *The Varieties of Religious Experience. op.cit.*, pp. 135-36.

[10]Ralph Barton Perry, *The Thought and Character of William James* (Little, Brown, and Co., 1935) Vol. I, p. 322.

[11]Henry James, Jr. (ed.), *The Letters of William James* (Boston: Atlantic Monthly Press, 1920), Vol. I, pp. 147-48.

[12]William James, "Is Life Worth Living?" *op.cit.*, p. 37.

[13]William James, *Pragmatism, op.cit.*, p. 38.

[14]Peirce nowhere coherently and completely articulated his approach to God. It must be gleaned from passing references in his collected writings. These gleanings are nowhere better assembled and commented on than in Charles Hartshorne and William Reese, *Philosophers Speak of God* (University of Chicago Press, 1963), pp. 258-69.

*CHAPTER SEVEN*

[1]"Natural Rights and the Theory of Political Institutions," *Mead: Selected Writings* (Bobbs-Merrill Co., Inc., 1964), p. 168.

[2]Robert O. Johann, *The Pragmatic Meaning of God* (Marquette University Press, 1966), p. 59.

[3]"Scientific Method and the Moral Sciences," Mead, *op.cit.*, p. 258.

[4]The most succinct and comprehensive statement by Mead of his overall philosophical position is contained in his article, "The Genesis of the Self and Social Control," *Mead,* op.cit., pp. 267-93.

*CHAPTER EIGHT*

[1]Gordon Kaufman, *God the Problem* (Harvard University Press, 1972), pp. 266-67.

[2]Paul Watzlawick, John Weakland, and Richard Fisch, *Change: Principles of Problem Formation and Problem Resolution* (W. W. Norton Co., Inc., 1974), p. 99.

[3]Ernest Becker, *The Denial of Death* (New York: The Free Press, 1973), pp. 203-04.

[4]William James, *The Will to Believe, op. cit.,* p. 24.

[5]Bertrand Russell, *Mysticism and Logic* (Longmans, Green and Co., 1918), pp. 56-57.

*CHAPTER NINE*

[1]Paul Ehrlich, *The End of Affluence* (Ballantine Books, 1974), p. 219.

[2]John Blofeld, *Beyond the Gods: Buddhist and Taoist Mysticism* (E. P. Dutton Co., Inc., 1974), p. 153.

[3]*Life* magazine (September 20, 1963).

[4]Meyer Friedman, M.D., and Ray H. Rosenman, M.D., *Type A Behavior and Your Heart* (Fawcett Publications, Inc., 1974), p. 84.

[5]See, for example, Van Meter Ames, *Zen and American Thought* (University of Hawaii Press, 1962); "Eastern Features in the Religious Philosophy of the Chicago School," *Proceedings of the IXth International Congress for the History of Religions* (August 1958) (Tokyo: Maruzen, 1960), pp. 475-80; "Aesthetic Values in the East and West," *The Journal of Aesthetics and Art Criticism* (Fall 1960), pp. 3-16; "William James and Zen," *Psychologia* (1959), pp. 114-19; "Art for Zen and Dewey," *Proceedings for the IVth International Congress on Aesthetics* (Athens, 1960), pp. 715-48.